The Creativity Factor

The Creativity Factor:

Unlocking the Potential of Your Team

Edward Glassman, Ph.D.

Pfeiffer
& COMPANY

San Diego • Toronto • Amsterdam • Sydney

Pfeiffer & Company
8517 Production Avenue
San Diego, California 92121
(619) 578-5900
FAX: (619) 578-2042

This book is printed on acid-free, recycled stock that meets or exceeds the
minimum GPO and EPA specifications for recycled paper.

This monograph is gratefully dedicated to:

Vicki Bradley, my special creative friend;
My parents who, in their own way,
encouraged me to write this book
when I was a child;
and THE GROUP who helped so much
and whose members know who they are.

Acknowledgments

Authors usually give credit to those who helped them with their writing. I have never fully understood the reason for this until now.

This book would not have been possible without the creative help, wisdom, and great effort of my editor, Florence Stone, group editor at American Management Association. She took my academic writing and helped turn it into readable (and even enjoyable) prose. I am extremely grateful for her selfless efforts on my behalf. She is a true editor/intrapreneur.

My creative friend, Vicki Bradley, has helped me in the presentation of numerous workshops over the past ten years. Much of the material in this book has come from these workshops and the countless discussions she and I have had about creativity, especially hers.

In 1983, I was a visiting fellow at the Center for Creative Leadership in Greensboro, North Carolina. Many people there helped to sow the seeds of this book. Some of these are: David Campbell, who inspired; Bob Dorn, who befriended; Bob Bailey, who clarified; Bill Drath, who helped me learn to write better; and David DeVries, who advised with wisdom. I am grateful to all of them.

Many managers and professionals read and gave me feedback on various versions of this book; to them I am very grateful. They are too numerous to mention, but their input appears on many of these pages.

Finally, I want to thank the thousands of people who attended my workshops and kindly gave me feedback on what worked and what needed improvement. Without their input, I could not have continually improved the workshop material that led to this book. I will always value and appreciate knowing them.

Edward Glassman

Foreword

To maintain global leadership it is essential that we out-think and out-perform our competitors. Our natural tendency is to tackle problems and opportunities by building from our long-standing experience base. This type of linear thinking is important and a logical starting point, particularly in team efforts in which team members have a diverse experience base. However, accomplishing revolutionary as well as evolutionary change often requires that we step outside our normal experience base and engage in non-linear thinking. For most people this is difficult. That's where the technology of creative thinking comes in. Many tools exist that force us outside our box of conventional thinking. That's what this book by Ed Glassman is all about.

According to Ed, who long ago was trained as a geneticist, the differences people display in the ability to think creatively are not inherited. Published research mentioned in Chapter 2 of this book using identical and fraternal twins supports this view. Creative thinking is a learnable skill. My experience in over twenty years as a director of research and development also reinforces this view. We have many examples in which step-change advances with bottom-line impact have derived from an individual or team practicing creative thinking tools of the type described in this book.

Ed Glassman has been a creativity-enhancing specialist consulting for Du Pont since 1983. He and others effectively teach the tools of creative thinking in seminars and as part of workshops designed to tackle practical problems. In this book, Ed describes many of these tools. He also touches on the creative climate that is necessary if creative ideas are to flourish and be implemented. Books like this are welcome additions to our library of important works in the newly formed Du Pont Center For Creativity and Innovation.

David Tanner, Director
Du Pont Center For Creativity
and Innovation
Wilmington, Delaware
February 1, 1991

Contents

Introduction

This book focuses on what works, not theory. I have presented workshops for more than fourteen years, and I have found that theory is interesting but what works is golden.

In 1983, while I was a visiting fellow at the Center for Creative Leadership in Greensboro, North Carolina, I was introduced to training in Creativity Procedures. Previously, I had a great deal of skepticism about learning to be more creative. After all, most of my colleagues had told me it could not be done. Also, I had not noticed any changes in my creativity over the past several decades. Nor had I seen any changes in creativity among my colleagues or students. My skepticism seemed well based in data.

In retrospect, the lack of creativity changes in these people, and in myself, now seems reasonable. After all, none of us knew *how* to improve our creativity skills, let alone that we *could*. We were caught in a vicious circle: Creativity couldn't be improved, so we ignored creativity improvement programs.

What changed my opinion?

While still at the Center, I began to develop a workshop on Creativity Procedures. Many of the participants reacted quite positively, including executives and managers from a diverse group of professions. I realized that creativity training could help anybody.

This book is for you, the team leader or team member committed to achieving excellence and renewal in your team. But what you gain from this book will depend on your willingness to plunge in and believe in what you are doing. What you gain will also depend on how well you involve your work group and how open you are to changing habits that can spoil creativity. The end result—solving problems more creatively—will depend on this.

I know of three sure-fire ways to improve creativity at work. First, use state-of-the-art Creativity Procedures so new ideas appear. Second, change the work climate so new ideas flourish. Finally, change approaches, so you stop pigeonholing yourself and other people; and provide a quick response with resources to test or implement new ideas.

You will find this and more in this book. You will find step-by-step instructions to carry out the activities essential to improving creativity. You will learn about problem-solving creativity meetings and how to motivate your team for more on-the-job creativity. You will come to terms with the habits and ideas that spoil creativity. And you will learn how to adjust your leadership style to encourage on-the-job creativity. But, as I said, your gain ultimately depends on the commitment you and your work group make to alter habits, apply new procedures, and change basic approaches to allow creativity and creative thinking to work for you as never before.

If you are like the people I have met in industry over the years, I think you will enjoy applying practical creativity to achieving excellence in your organization. And you and the people in your work group will enjoy work more than ever.

Edward Glassman
Chapel Hill, North Carolina

Chapter 1

"If You Always Do What You Have Always Done, You Will Always Get What You Have Always Gotten"

Creativity is defined as the ability to generate new and useful ideas. Many eons ago, a pre-human being had the first creative thought and produced the first new and useful idea. And we humans have been doing it ever since, with the most glorious results.

How do we do it? Is it by free association, intuition, meditation, "remote associations"? Who knows? We are still quite ignorant about how the brain functions. But it is fortunate that it works so well.

It now can also work better.

A Quiet Revolution

For the past fifty years or so, a quiet revolution in Creativity Procedures has been taking place. A great change has occurred in the way we can produce new and useful ideas. No longer do we have to wait to have a new and useful idea by free association, intuition, meditation, "remote associations," or by whatever means the brain churns out a new and useful idea. Now we have hundreds of Creativity Procedures to help us produce new and useful ideas and solve problems creatively.

"Hold on," you say. "Didn't those old techniques work for thousands of years to produce new and useful ideas? Didn't we construct our entire civilization using those old ways? What do we need new Creativity Procedures for? If it ain't broke, do you want to go around fixing it?"

Of course, waiting around to stumble on a new and useful idea still works—and works very well indeed. We constructed our entire civilization this way. And I wouldn't want to change that one bit. Hurrah for heroic creativity! But the revolution in Creativity Procedures speeded up the process, and we now can produce more useful ideas in a shorter time. And because we have more ideas to choose from, the quality of the final solution is much better.

Ask any team trained in brainstorming. Its biggest complaint is that it has trouble sorting and selecting ideas. Imagine! The problem is no

3

longer how to generate enough new and useful ideas, but rather how to sort and select from all the ideas generated. How sweet it is to move from the dilemma of fifty years ago—having too few ideas—to the current situation of having to evaluate the myriad ideas a simple brainstorming session produces.

And brainstorming, which was invented over fifty years ago, when the Model A Ford was in use, isn't the most modern development, either. Using only brainstorming is like getting around in a Model A Ford or a DC-3 airplane. Not using up-to-date Creativity Procedures is like ignoring computers, TV, fax machines, and all the other modern inventions from which we benefit.

The Old Versus the New

Suppose you had an important twenty-page report and had to get it to a city about two hundred miles away as soon as possible. Here are some ways you could do this:

- You could put on your running outfit and run as fast as you can, or you could use a horse;
- You might send it by first-class mail;
- You might send it by overnight air delivery;
- You might get in a car, airplane, or on a train and carry it there;
- You might dictate the report over the telephone;
- You might fax it.

Obviously, if speed were essential, you would want to raise the probability that the report would get there as soon as possible. Hence you would fax it. You wouldn't use the other choices because the probabilities are that they would be much slower. Yet that's what most people do when solving problems. While seeking the highest quality solution, they use methods with the lowest probability of achieving that. Not using modern Creativity Procedures to solve problems is like running two hundred miles to deliver the report instead of using the fax machine.

Old-fashioned unstructured free-association procedures have the lowest probability of achieving a high-quality creative solution. That's not because they are poor approaches, but rather because the new Creativity Procedures are so much better. These include Targeted Free Association, Forced Combinations, Metaphors, Analogies, and Future Fantasy. These new Creativity Procedures raise the probability that outstanding creative outcomes will happen.

Before discussing some of these procedures, let's look at some myths about creativity and examine the problem-solving process as a whole.

Chapter 2

Creativity as a Learnable Skill

I was a professor of biochemistry and genetics at the University of North Carolina for many years, and one of the recurring questions in my research was, "Is creativity inherited?" After all, if creativity is inherited like I.Q., then little can be done to help an uncreative person.

Some Creativity Skills

Here are some important creativity skills. Are they inherited?

- The ability to associate remote stimuli in the environment with elements in the mind and combine them into new and unusual ideas;

- The ability to keep an open mind and see new perspectives;

- The ability to generate many ideas;

- The ability to adopt many different problem-solving approaches;

- The ability to generate a variety of really different ideas;

- The ability to develop ideas;

- The ability to generate infrequent and uncommon ideas.

- The ability to hang in there when going against consensus and to be persistent in the face of criticism.

Few of the creativity skills listed above seem to me to be inheritable; instead, most seem learnable. Indeed, research on how identical and fraternal twins score on tests of these creativity skills demonstrates this. Many research studies show that differences between the scores of identical twins on creativity tests are similar to the differences between the scores of fraternal twins. Therefore, these creativity skills do not have a large genetic contribution.

This is good news indeed. If these creativity skills were inherited, this book would end now with a statement like, "Sorry, what you have is what you will always have, and learning new Creativity Procedures will not help." But the opposite is true. Most people can learn to be more creative.

To accept this is to escape from a major myth about creativity that can lead to a self-fulfilling prophecy: Nothing can harm a highly creative person, and nothing can help an uncreative person. Not so on both counts.

First, most creativity skills are not inherited, as shown by the research on identical and fraternal twins.

Second, most Creativity Procedures can be learned.

Third, creativity is greatly affected by the job environment and other external factors.

Finally, success as a creative person depends not only on creativity skills but on motivation and interpersonal skills.

Most of us have creative ability and use it every day. We just don't recognize it as creativity. We call it tinkering, ingenuity, fooling around, intuition, trial and error, imagination, problem solving, inventing—anything but creativity. But the ongoing process of generating new and useful ideas to solve problems at work is creativity. And much can be done to improve this process, involving people in your work group to solve problems more effectively.

Another Creativity Myth

Some people think that the first step, that is, the generation of the big-bang idea, is the only role that creativity plays in the innovation processes. This is another myth. Creativity is needed to solve problems throughout the entire process of innovation. We need to realize that on-the-job creativity and creative thinking are daily, ongoing processes of transforming old ideas into new and that Creativity Procedures are important in all steps in the innovation process. And that's not all.

Using Creativity to Achieve Excellence

Today, many companies have found that creativity is important in winning a competitive edge. They use Creativity Procedures to solve problems in marketing, manufacturing, R&D, human resources, purchasing, strategic planning, cost cutting, finance, productivity, quality control, computer effectiveness, sales, new product development, and developing patents.

Creativity at work is a daily activity that involves the ability to change perspective and generate new and useful ideas. Although training in applied Creativity Procedures does not turn out Einsteins, it does help people learn how to find better solutions to problems. For example, after attending one of my creativity workshops, a manager from a Fortune 500 company asked me to help him creatively solve some problems in a new area of business recently assigned to him. He had approached the assignment in the usual, time-worn ways and wanted to develop some creative ideas.

We arranged a creativity meeting with fifteen people from his company: five from R&D, five from marketing, and five from manufacturing. After one and a half days of using Creativity Procedures, he had several hundred ideas; fifteen individual one-page "trigger proposals," one from each participant; and fifteen people whom he could use as helpful resources. He later wrote me, "One of the approaches identified at the workshop has been picked up and should be commercialized shortly. We have had a very positive response from a major retail chain."

If you want your team to produce more profitable products and services and to use better processes and procedures than the ones that it is now using, then you and your team need to start using new Creativity Procedures.

Chapter 3

What Is On-the-Job Creativity?

How we humans do this wondrous activity called creativity is not known, but there are some intriguing notions. One suggests that creative solutions are triggered by chance events that bring together diverse elements of the mind into one thought and force them into new combinations that are useful. This process has been called "making remote associations."

This theory suggests the need for a prepared, active mind full of diverse elements that can combine to form a creative idea to solve a particular problem. As Pasteur pointed out, chance favors the prepared mind.

Thus, creativity is the combining of old information and old ideas into new ideas that are useful. This concept certainly runs contrary to the myth that creativity is the creation of ideas out of nothing. Solving problems creatively is a down-to-earth activity, not a mountain-top phenomenon. You don't have to be special to use Creativity Procedures to solve problems creatively.

The Stages in the Creative Process

Here are the stages of the creative process:

Preparation. Fact finding. Laying the groundwork and learning the background. Learning Creativity Procedures.

Concentration. Total absorption in the problem.

Incubation. Taking time out. Seeking distractions. Working on other things.

Illumination. "Aha!" The idea pops out.

Implementation. Solving practical problems of implementation. Getting other people involved.

The preparation stage can last many years: in school, on-the-job training, reading, taking courses, traveling, living, etc. After all, you cannot be a creative chemist, a creative engineer, or a creative computer whiz unless you know chemistry, engineering, or computers. You have to learn your craft and profession first.

During the concentration stage, you focus on a particular problem, making a place in your mind for a new idea to enter.

Frustration at not finding a solution leads to the incubation stage, during which time you concentrate on other things while your mind takes a break and quietly makes remote associations.

Then, if you are lucky, the illumination stage takes place, the "aha" insight forms, and a new, useful idea emerges.

This leads to the implementation stage where the entire process cycles to modify and use the new idea.

Thus, new ideas do not appear spontaneously out of the blue. They require preparation, concentration, incubation, and the appropriate trigger to spark new remote associations.

These notions trigger a number of questions for you and your work group:

- How much incubation time is built into team members' weekly schedules?

- Is "doing" more highly valued than "thinking"? Is it okay for people to spend time thinking?

- How much time is allotted to the preparation stage to get diverse elements into people's minds?

- How are diverse elements in the mind obtained? By travel? Reading? Meetings? Training? Conventions? Trade fairs? Talking to customers, suppliers, competitors, people in other companies, in foreign lands, in other professions? Is this encouraged by you and your work group?

If yours is like most work groups, you'll find that not enough time is allotted to the incubation phase of the creative process. Another creativity-spoiling habit: People are not deliberately encouraged to increase the number of diverse elements in their mind.

Bizarre Trigger Ideas Can Spark Better Ideas

Creativity means that ideas are useful as well as original. Still, all ideas can be used as stepping stones to more useful ideas.

For example, consider the statement: "Let's train bears to climb telephone poles in winter and shake off the ice that breaks the transmission wires." This idea was allegedly proposed to prevent ice from breaking power lines in a mountain region where winters are cold and rainy. One of the technicians had complained about being harassed by bears on a repair trip. This led one person, in a spirit of fun, to suggest training bears to climb the poles and shake the ice loose, clearly a bizarre idea.

A second person, again in jest, suggested putting pots of honey on the tops of the poles in winter so the bears would climb the poles and shake the ice off the wires, another bizarre idea. A third person suggested, still in fun, using helicopters to place the pots of honey on the poles to attract the bears, also a bizarre idea.

Yet this led to a solution I am told is still being used. The down draft from helicopters flying over the wires knocks the ice off.

Obviously, this story has been embellished with each retelling. Still, it has a kernel of truth and a great deal of wisdom. It exemplifies my point that bizarre ideas can trigger practical, useful solutions. Not all such trigger ideas spark useful solutions, but unless you encourage and help bizarre ideas to survive, much creativity is lost.

Linear and Non-Linear Creativity Procedures

There are lots of ways to get new and useful ideas. One way is using linear Creativity Procedures. It is the most used way because of its low risk. I can demonstrate it to you this way:

$$A \rightarrow B \rightarrow C \rightarrow D \rightarrow \text{New and Useful Idea}$$

Each step is carefully checked for truth, logic, and wisdom before moving to the next. It is very precise and analytical and very certain. You know where you are heading, how to get there, when you get there, and why you wanted to be there in the first place.

Does it work? You can be sure it does. Most of our rational thinking is based on this model. It is similar to the scientific method. Much of our world was constructed using this creative approach.

But another way to get new and useful ideas is with non-linear Creativity Procedures. Ideas leap from A to Z to R to E to X...and eventually out of bizarre trigger ideas some new and useful ideas may emerge.

Now this is clearly a very uncertain process. You do not know where you are heading, how you will get there, when you get there, or even why you wanted to be there in the first place. It is very risky, unpredictable, and ambiguous. Often it leads nowhere. But when a new and useful idea emerges, it is very likely to be unique.

Let's look again at the train of thought in the non-linear creativity that turned the bears and the pots of honey into helicopters.

1. Technician reports being harassed by bears;
2. Bears trained to climb poles and shake ice off wires;
3. Pots of honey placed on tops of poles to attract bears to climb and shake wires;
4. Helicopters used to place honey on tops of poles to attract bears;
5. The down blast of helicopters used to remove ice from wires.

None of these bizarre ideas logically led to the other, yet the outcome was quite useful. Note that had the process been terminated along the way by anyone at the meeting insisting on serious ideas only, the useful outcome would never have occurred.

This leads us to another creativity-spoiling habit: We don't deliberately misperceive the world to obtain a creative viewpoint.

Chapter 4

Testing Your Creativity Habits

I have a friend who has a constant, gentle wit, whose humor often turns out to be quite helpful in discussions that are getting too tense. "Everyone thinks I'm funny," he says. "Actually, I'm out of control." My own observations lead me to the same conclusion. He says almost anything that comes to his mind—he is extremely spontaneous.

Generally, we do not let ourselves act spontaneously, even for a moment. We relentlessly inhibit spontaneity and repress our wit and humor. Do you do this? Each of us has the ability to be far more creative than we ever suspected. A bit of fun here will prove this.

Add one line to this and turn it into a 6:

IX

Take this seriously but remember to have some fun at the same time. Spend no less than three or four minutes on this problem before moving on (no peeking ahead, please).

In fact, there are several solutions to this problem, the most common of which is to add an S to the IX to produce SIX. If you got this, congratulations—but actually I am more interested if you got a different answer or no answer at all.

If you got no answer, what do you suppose blocked your mind? Most people in my workshops say that they thought I meant a straight line, or that they forgot numbers can be words, or that they were looking for Roman numerals.

Essentially, our thoughts get stuck in collectors within our minds and cannot get out. I call these collectors *mind funnels*. Once you get stuck in a specific mind funnel, it becomes almost impossible to get out—unless you use Creativity Procedures. Every time a new but related problem arises, you'll return to the same mind funnel that succeeded before. But by sticking every problem into the old mind funnel, you can wind up with the same timeworn solution. And each time this happens, the mind funnel gets bigger, and the ability to explore other perspectives becomes more remote. Instead, you exert all your effort into pushing the problem through that mind funnel to find an adequate solution.

To get the answer S + IX → SIX, you need to pass through at least two mind funnels, one that tells you numbers can be words, and another that tells you lines can be curved. But there are other, less obvious and equally correct solutions:

- Add a 6 since 1 x 6 equals 6;

- Add a thick line over the top half of the IX (thus ▆) and turn it upside down (VI);

- Move one line of the X to the left to form a distorted VI.

- Fold the paper through the IX and turn it over so that all you see is VI.

The last two solutions may disturb you because I said, "add a line" and none was added. In fact, mind funnels are at work here. It could be *fairness* ("You said to add a line"), or it could be you are *making unwarranted assumptions* ("You never said we could fold the paper").

But why do solutions to problems have to be "fair"—why must they always fit stated conditions and preconceived notions? Why do we make unwarranted assumptions about problems without checking out their validity? How often do you find yourself doing this at work?

More on Mind Funnels

Mind funnels are triggered by words, remote associations, visual impressions, and ideas, among other elements. They can keep us glued to the past. Used over and over again, they keep us from examining current successes and ultimately are responsible for another creativity spoiler, the *quick fix.*

The quick fix allows us to accept the first adequate solution to a problem instead of exploring new and potentially better solutions. It is all too common in the workplace.

How can you avoid the quick fix? One way is to set a *quota* of three to five really different ideas before choosing one. Or hold a mini-brainstorming session and list *all* the ideas, realistic and bizarre, you come up with over three to five minutes.

One habit associated with the quick fix is to rush to generate solutions before defining the problem. Often, problems may find their way into the wrong mind funnels. As time passes, these mind funnels get larger, and they become more divergent from current reality. A successful mind funnel is called a perspective; unsuccessful funnels are simply ruts. And as you use mind funnels, chances are you do not explore to determine the entire range of possible new ideas within them. Nor do you look for new mind funnels that could be useful in solving problems. Creativity Procedures can help here.

Even if you are open to new ideas, though, you cannot expect them to develop or surface if you set time constraints. Creativity takes time. If I ask you for all the solutions you can find to a particular problem and limit your solution time to five minutes, you may come up with good solutions—but how many more might you come up with if you have one hour or if there are no time constraints on your creativity?

Moreover, you can and should share the information within various mind funnels. Often, by putting together diverse bits of information, you can find a new and innovative solution to a problem.

This can be carried into the workplace by encouraging your team to work together to solve problems creatively. The more creativity groups that are formed, the better. This is not a waste, because from many creativity groups you can gather a diversity of high-quality ideas and solutions.

Also, it is restrictive to list criteria before you have new ideas. Let the ideas come first, then identify the criteria. There are no good or bad ideas, just ideas that do or do not fit your criteria. But if you box in your thinking on the basis of established criteria, you may never even bother to formulate your ideas. Generate the ideas first. Let your imagination soar.

Some Creative Thinking

How many ways do you think there are to represent half of eight? Write down the number here____.

Now list all the ways you can think of to represent half of eight. Spend at least ten minutes before you move on.

Here are some of the ways people in my creativity workshops have represented half of eight:

Mathematical mind funnels: 1 x 4, 2 x 2, 3 x 1.25, 4 x 1, etc.; 2^2, $\sqrt{\sqrt{6}}$, $2\sqrt{4}$, $4\sqrt{1}$, etc.; and 1 + 3, 2 + 2, 3 + 1, 5 - 1, 6 - 2, etc.

Mind funnels that slice "8" in half: o and o are the top and bottom halves of eight; E and 3 are the left and right halves of 8. If you use this mind funnel, you can halve the 8 in all directions, leading to an infinity of answers. Indeed, you might get into a more general mind funnel and halve all representations of eight in an infinite number of ways. This can be done not only on 8, but on eight, VIII, and other ways to represent eight.

Mind funnels to write four: Four, 4, IV, 1111, etc. Use ideographs to represent four in Chinese, Japanese, Sanskrit, Hindu, and Ancient Egyptian.

Mind funnels using codes for four: 100 (binary numbers), 11 (ternary numbers), etc.; Morse or Semaphore codes; deaf sign language; boat pennant representing 4; + + + + sign of the four (from the Sherlock Holmes story); 500 (1000 is the binary number for 8; one-half of this is 500); 10 and 00 (cutting 1000 in half); VI and II (cutting VIII in half).

Other mind funnels: Show four fingers (like a four-year old does when asked his or her age); 7:30 (the German halb acht); hit the ground four times with your leg (what Clever Hans, the horse, did when asked what half of eight was). Here's one idea involving sound as a mind funnel: I am told "4" has a universal frequency within most phone companies and represents half of eight in sound all over the world.

Now imagine you are in my creativity workshop, and you only hear me say, "List all the ways to represent half of 8." Remember, that was not written, just heard. Would you get into the following mind funnel: "Half of ate"? And if you did, how would you use it? Would you write "hungry," or draw a half-eaten apple or an apple cut into pieces?

Learning About Your Mind Funnels from "Half of Eight/Ate"

Much can be learned. First, numerous and diverse mind funnels exist for all problems, even one as seemingly obvious as how to represent half of eight, and certainly for the many problems we take for granted as we attempt to solve them at work. Yet, we blithely continue the quick fix, ignoring rich possibilities. You say you don't have time to explore enriching possibilities at work. That is another creativity spoiler: Not allotting enough time to explore different mind funnels.

In my creativity workshop, many solutions are suggested, yet each person discovers only a few. The lesson is clear: One of the reasons for working in groups is the sharing of mind funnels. Each person has unique knowledge and experience, and therefore his or her mind funnels are unique and valuable. (Later we will examine procedures to ensure effective sharing of mind funnels and perspectives in creative teams.)

So, do not rush when solving problems. A hasty early choice leads to overlooking rich new possibilities. Creativity takes time and often means communicating with other people to discover new mind funnels.

Chapter 5

Helping New Ideas Flourish in Your Work Group

How do you usually react to new ideas from people in your work group? Do you weigh various options and objections, or do you automatically say, "No"? Do you act immediately or wait for months before acting on a new idea? Do you accept ideas but offer no rewards—not even a pat on the back? Ask yourself honestly what you really do with new ideas.

The answer is important, for how you respond to new ideas impacts the creativity of your work group.

It's very easy to squelch creativity. A little criticism can do it. Disinterest in the form of a delayed response can do it, too. Such responses cause people to suppress their ideas and ideas are lost. Your most creative people will stop being creative on the job and save their creativity for the weekends. They may become defensive and even withhold or shoot down their own ideas before you do. When creativity isn't nurtured, people will do things the same old safe, complacent way instead of taking risks, exploring new mind funnels, and developing half-baked, half-developed, bizarre ideas into useful ones.

You don't want this to happen, and you can make sure it doesn't. You are responsible for promoting the creativity of those in your work group. Why? Because you encourage or discourage creativity just in how you respond to the ideas of other people.

Avoiding the Automatic "No"

I advocate three responses to ideas. The first is known as I.P.N.C., which stands for **I**nterest, **P**ositive, **N**egative, and **C**uriosity. It delays voicing negative comments that are expressed as concerns.

The second approach I advocate is called "Yes, if...." Curbing an automatic "No" and responding to a new idea with "Yes, if...." gives you a chance to visualize the conditions necessary to get from "No" to "Yes." You can also create a positive, idea-nurturing climate.

One executive I know who used this approach for the first time said that it not only kept him from using his automatic "No" but also led him to really listen and analyze ideas to see how he could help move from "No" to "Yes." "It converted me into a collaborator, who helps a new idea get going, instead of a judge."

The third approach is Idea Improvement Analysis (I.I.A.). Each aspect of an idea is rated on a scale of one to ten, and anything with a low rating is considered a handicap to overcome rather than a reason for rejection. This process usually generates discussions that help new ideas instead of bogging them down with negativism.

Let's assume someone approached you with a drawing and said, "Here's a great design that'll make us a lot of money." How would you respond?

First, remember that the new idea must have some merit. After all, its proposer thinks so. And remember that you want members of your work group to bring you their ideas in the future. You also do not want to make this person feel rejected or resentful. You want to create a constructive atmosphere where he or she can tell you about the design without feeling pressured or defensive.

Given these considerations, you do not want to say, "That's a lousy design." Instead, you can use I.P.N.C. to extol the virtues of the design but also to voice concern about some aspects.

"Yes, if...." could be used in the same way, to let the idea's merits show fully. You could rate the idea with I.I.A. and give some elements of the design a low rating, but you could also say, "How can we overcome this?" instead of giving a blanket "No."

Quick Creativity Spoilers

Don't resort to what I call quick creativity spoilers. Don't say, "We've never done it that way before," or "Someone would have suggested it before if it were any good," or "It just won't work." Don't claim that it would be unfeasible from a budgetary standpoint or that it would be politically unsuitable. And certainly don't use the time-honored death knell, "Let's form a committee."

When you come out with comments like these, you discourage people from sharing their ideas. Creative people then stop being creative in the office, saving their creativity, as I mentioned, for the weekend. No one explores new mind funnels. You may be safe in such an environment, but as someone once said, "You have to help many caterpillars if you want to be around butterflies." Always remember: "Creativity help leads to more creativity help, while lack of support leads to more lack of support."

Modeling the Right Behavior

As you work to foster a climate for creativity, you will stimulate others to do likewise. You will see signs of improved receptiveness in your team members. A positive creative climate is a rarity. It takes a great deal of courage to stand up for someone else's ideas. It takes courage to defer the judgment of ideas you think are not useful. But you must convince your team members to do just that by modeling the behaviors you want to encourage. You must make the "What's *good* about this?" approach the habitual one, not the "It won't work" attitude.

Help Idea Submissions

And don't stop there. Make clear how you feel about creative efforts by truly rewarding creativity.

Many organizations talk about creativity but do not reward creative efforts. Nor do they provide the creative person with the support he or she needs to submit a fully developed idea, clarify what is needed for an idea to be positively received, or reward the innovator with the opportunity to do the project, if desired. No wonder such organizations suffer from lack of creativity.

If you want creativity, make sure the rewards for creative efforts are equal to, or exceed, those for good performance on approved projects. Emphasize the submission of new ideas in job descriptions and performance reviews and in the reward process. And give the creative person the assistance he or she needs to develop the idea for team review, and implement it if that's what the person wants to do.

Chapter 6

Solving Problems More Creatively: A Problem-Solving Sequence to Follow

There is a problem-solving sequence that works well to produce creative solutions:

Step 1: Define the problem and list many problem statements.

Step 2: Identify criteria to select the final problem statement.

Step 3: Select reasonable problem statements.

Step 4: List many ideas.

Step 5: Identify criteria to select ideas.

Step 6: Combine ideas into creative trigger-proposals and workable solutions.

Of these six steps, the most critical creative steps are the first, fourth, and sixth. These will be discussed in the next three chapters. But here I'd like to examine the process itself.

This sequence combines two important concepts essential to solving problems creatively.

First, it keeps you from rushing to generate solutions before you have carefully defined the problem—to make sure you are solving the right problem. It keeps you from stuffing the new problem into a comfortable, old thought pattern.

People who spend more time on Step 1 usually produce more creative solutions than people who rush to Step 4 first. This makes a great deal of sense since jolting your mind first to pursue new directions and new mind funnels will ensure that you generate different types of ideas. You will wind up in a different place than you would have had you continued moving down a comfortable old rut.

Second, the sequence prevents you from identifying criteria first— another habit we all have. When you do that, you box in your creativity. All the subsequent statements or ideas are prematurely evaluated.

Sometimes we are given criteria to use to solve a problem. Or we carry unstated or phantom criteria in our minds. These, too, can inhibit creativity for they box us in.

To keep the impact of criteria under control during the problem-solving process, all stated and unstated criteria need to be dealt with openly. This procedure is helpful:

1. Non-evaluatively list all given and unstated criteria. Set a quota for listing at least ten to twenty phantom criteria;

2. Reverse the criteria. Distort them. Shrink them. Magnify them. Play "What if?" games with them. Do whatever you can do to open your mind and get away from the criteria.

Later, when you have finished generating ideas, you can return to the criteria to select ideas that fit.

Now let's look at the three key steps in the problem-solving process, beginning with Step 1: defining the problem.

Chapter 7

Define Problems Creatively: The First Key Creative Step

Defining the problem is essential. Too often we spend time solving the wrong problem because we haven't really given enough consideration to the situation.

To prevent this from happening you should generate a long list of diverse problem statements prior to idea generation. This will open up a broad range of perspectives, a key step in solving problems creatively. The more difficult the situation, the more time should be spent in this phase.

Set up a group meeting. Different perspectives on the original problem statement are more likely to surface in groups because of the unique experiences and thought patterns that each person brings to the problem.

It will also help if you start your problem statements with the words "how to." This will keep you from getting into discussions of solutions too soon in the problem.

Stimulating "How-To" Thinking

The following are some phrases that should stimulate your thinking as you develop your how-to statement:

How to gain, how to improve, how to change, how to add, how to fix, how to minimize, how to accomplish, how to enhance, how to cope with, how to restore, how to do away with, how to produce, how to exceed, how to maximize, how to reduce, how to deliver, how to make best use of, how to handle, how to change, how to develop, how to control, and how to launch.

Also, how to alter, how to switch, how to admire, how to begin, how to plan, how to revive, how to upgrade, how to arrange, how to enrich, how to start, how to expand, how to build, how to manage, how to commence, how to enlarge, how to establish, how to succeed, how to attempt, how to adapt, how to originate, how to schedule, how to grow, how to learn to, how to perform, how to make, how to end, how to destroy, and how to inspire.

Also, how to motivate, how to deal with, how to conquer, how to modify, how to challenge, how to reward, how to satisfy, how to establish, how to afford, how to increase, how to reject, how to persuade, how to enrich, how to encourage, how to invent, how to create, how to innovate, how to enjoy, how to appreciate, how to achieve, how to tell, how to share, how to distribute, how to assemble, how to reverse, how to twist, how to blend, how to combine, how to interchange, how to substitute, how to rearrange, how to use, how to give, how to substantiate, and how to move forward.

Gaining New Perspectives

There are a number of Creativity Procedures that can be used to help you discover new mind funnels and generate how-to statements that reflect new perspectives on a problem situation. Let's look at some of these.

Reverse Assumptions. This method helps you deal with unwarranted assumptions about a problem. You begin by non-evaluatively listing five to twenty basic assumptions about your problem. Include especially obvious assumptions you take for granted—ones you don't even consider anymore. Next, reverse the meaning of these assumptions. Then, non-evaluatively force combinations between your reversed assumptions and your how-to statement. Select, combine, change, add to, and work over your ideas to come up with many new problem statements.

Like-Improve Analysis. Describe your problem. Now look at what you like and what you don't like about the description. Dissect out what you want to improve. Writing the information down as you proceed will greatly improve the quality of the final how-to problem statement.

Guided Fresh Eye. This method encourages you to think about the problem situation as if you were someone or something else. Begin with the problem statement. Now rewrite the problem as if you were a dolphin, bat, eagle, jellyfish, pea pod, or oak seed (choose one); or chemical engineer, mechanical engineer, Martian, or artist (again, choose one); or biologist, chemist, secretary, banker, frog or pharmacologist (choose one); and so forth. Now restate the problem. You'll see new perspectives.

Word Substitution. Word substitution can effectively transform how-to problem statements. Systematically change key nouns, verbs, and adverbs to help you switch track in your creative thinking. For example, you can transform "How to get rid of an autocratic leader" into "How to abolish...," "How to work with...," "How to change...," "How to succeed with...," "How to enjoy...," "How to flourish with...," etc. Note the different perspectives that occur with each word substitution.

Who, What, Where, When, and Why. This method asks the questions that force you to look at a problem in a different way. First, you write a problem statement. You then attempt to answer the following questions about the problem: Why? Who? What? Where? When? Now restate the problem. See if answering these questions hasn't given you new insights.

Needs, Obstacles, and Constraints. This method forces you to look at a problem in a different way. You begin by writing a problem statement. Then you non-evaluatively list your needs; that is, what you want to achieve or gain. Next, you list the obstacles or things in your way that need to be overcome. Finally, you list the constraints—things you must accept or cope with. All this will change your perspective on the problem.

Weaknesses of Quick-Fix Solutions. This method asks you to list four quick-fix solutions and the weaknesses of each. Now rewrite the problem statement based on what has been learned from the analyses of the quick fixes.

Targeted Analogies and Metaphors Based on the Problem's Essence. The mere mention of a problem can generate myriad thoughts and pictures in your mind that are hard to avoid and thus spoil creativity. Here's a method that should help you put these thoughts out of your mind as you consider the situation.

In the first step, deal only with an action verb that captures the essence of the problem. For example, the "essence" or action verb of an auto jack is *lifting* things; the wheelbarrow is *transporting* things; walking on water is *floating* things or *freezing* water.

In the second step, generate examples of the problem's essence as metaphors and analogies from the plant and animal world; from industry and government; from various professions; from other countries; from ethnic and religious groups; from the historical past; from mythical and exotic world places, and so forth.

In the third step, choose one interesting example and list detailed characteristics and properties of the example.

In the fourth step, force combinations between these characteristics to provide exotic, bizarre ideas.

Finally, improve and develop each bizarre idea into realistic, sensible, workable problem statements. One way to do this is to non-evaluatively list each characteristic, property, nuance, and free association as you consider the bizarre idea. Force combinations between these and the problem.

Analogies and metaphors like these can get you thinking along new lines and new mind funnels so you will wind up in new places.

Identify Criteria to Select Problem Statements.

Take a sheet of paper and answer the following: Whose problem is it? What kind of problem is it (marketing, technological, financial, etc.)? How big is the problem? Then list your own gut feelings, as well as tangible and intangible values. This, or a variation, may help you create a final problem statement.

Once you have settled on a problem statement, you are ready to generate creative ideas—the second key creative step in the process.

Chapter 8

Generate New Ideas Abundantly: The Second Key Creative Step

Discovering new approaches and generating creative ideas to solve a problem is a probabilities game. No matter what you do, there is no guarantee that creative outcomes will occur.

Still, if you use the Creativity Procedures identified in this chapter and change your habits and the creative climate in your mind and around you, you will surely raise the probability that a useful outcome will occur.

Let's now look at some Creativity Procedures to generate ideas abundantly and solve problems creatively.

Untargeted Free Association

Untargeted Free Association is used when the trigger ideas for idea generation are not stated. It is a mystery how we do this. Still, this is how we usually get new ideas. The remote associations sparked by Untargeted Free Association are generally less creative, however, than those from "Targeted Free Association," "Forced Combinations," and "Future Fantasy," all of which are described below.

Targeted Free Association

Brainstorming. This was invented over fifty years ago, and newer and more effective technologies to enhance idea generation for groups and individuals have been developed since then. Still, brainstorming, when carried out correctly, provides an excellent opportunity to record your pet ideas so you won't forget them, flush out obvious ideas from your mind, and clear the way for creativity with newer, more advanced Creativity Procedures.

During brainstorming, ideas are called out in a group of five to seven people where status differences are small, and a recorder writes the ideas on a note pad or flip chart for all to see. This generally produces lots of ideas, some unique and of high quality.

There are a number of useful variations. One is to brainstorm for three minutes, be quiet for three minutes, brainstorm for another three minutes, and so forth. Another is to go around a group in order, allowing people to pass.

Since there is no anonymity of ideas with brainstorming, many people hold back. To increase the number of ideas expressed, Osborn (1963), the inventor of brainstorming, insisted on following these guidelines:

Suspend judgment. Postpone evaluation and defer judgment until later.

Freewheel. The wilder the idea, the better. It is easier to tame down than to think up.

Quantity. The greater the number of ideas, the greater the likelihood of producing one that is innovative and useful.

Cross-fertilize. Combine and piggyback ideas. You can use trigger-ideas to spark still better ideas.

Perhaps most important to brainstorming is *non-evaluative listing.* There are many reasons to postpone evaluation. Obviously, one is to encourage people to express ideas. But equally important, the basis for evaluation is old information and old criteria. When we evaluate, we immerse our thinking in old, time-worn approaches. So, to escape from old approaches, we need to be non-evaluative.

Toward this, list all ideas. Do not discuss items or ask questions. Do not evaluate or make fun of suggestions. Repetition is okay. Do not reject an item because it is already listed. Neither the recorder nor group members have to understand or like the items listed. Questions for clarification come later. Defer judgment and postpone evaluations until later. Just keep the process moving.

Buzz Groups. This procedure uses little time and is one antidote to the quick fix during meetings. It is especially useful when someone wants to get a lot of ideas in a meeting without precipitating a full discussion. Here's how this procedure works:

One person presents a problem. Then groups of four to six people turn in their seats to form small Buzz Groups right where they sit. After quickly choosing a recorder, each group non-evaluatively lists as many ideas on 8½″ x 11″ paper as they can in four to five minutes. These are quickly read to the presenter of the problem, who is also given a copy of the written list of ideas for future use. If the problem-presenter merely says "thank you" and does not get trapped into a discussion of the ideas, the total time spent can be less than fifteen minutes.

One variation of this is first to ask the Buzz Groups to non-evaluatively list how-to problem statements. Then one or more of these are chosen by the presenter of the problem for the Buzz Groups to use during idea generation.

A true story: A plant manager from a Fortune 500 company at one of my workshops told of a situation in which management wanted to restructure work units to eliminate supervisors and have the groups of workers led by group leaders. Everyone was in favor of the idea but the union, which insisted that everyone get the same raise as the group leaders, especially since the supervisory position was to be phased out.

We formed three Buzz Groups from the eighteen people present, and while they were non-evaluatively listing ideas, the plant manager and I agreed that the most we could expect were some trigger-ideas to spark ideas at a later time. Consequently, we were surprised to receive over forty ideas, three of which, when combined, yielded a solution that would not only satisfy the union but, because of its incentive orientation, would increase productivity while reducing supervisory costs.

Brainwriting

By 1970, research had shown that groups of people who sat quietly listing their ideas on their own pad of paper generated more ideas than a comparable group of people brainstorming. This finding led to the development of Brainwriting.

This procedure can be carried out in small or large groups. Since the ideas are anonymous, people generally do not hold ideas back as much as in brainstorming. But the ideas generated, while numerous, often lack breadth, because no perspectives are exchanged as in brainstorming. However, Brainwriting can be combined with brainstorming for multiple benefits.

The basis for most Brainwriting procedures is *automatic writing*. I learned this procedure from Bill Drath at the Center for Creative Leadership.

In automatic writing you write down all thoughts triggered. Do not hold back. Orderly thoughts are not required. Correct grammar is unimportant. Incomplete phrases are fine. There is also no effort at evaluation. Thoughts are allowed to flow directly onto paper. Nor do thoughts have to fit the topic (that would box you in).

When stuck, you are encouraged to write, "I have nothing to write" until you do have something to write.

I use automatic writing when I am stuck in my thinking or my writing. It almost always allows interesting ideas to emerge.

Automatic writing is a valuable Creativity Procedure that you can use to help list problem statements as well as solve problems creatively.

Here are a number of Brainwriting procedures to follow:

Idea Gallery Brainwriting. Here, you write the six to ten problem statements that are of greatest interest on flip-chart paper, one problem statement per sheet. Attach the flip-chart papers to the wall. Then people walk around the room and write ideas and solutions directly on the papers. The ideas that accumulate on the papers frequently trigger ideas in other people as they wander around. The physical activity often also helps to stimulate creativity.

Use this procedure by hanging a paper with a problem statement written at the top outside your office door, inviting people to write their ideas. Some really useful ideas will appear.

Idea Card Brainwriting. During Idea Card Brainwriting each person quietly reflects on the problem, mulls over new thoughts, and privately writes ideas for about thirty or forty minutes on 5" or 8" colored index cards with a dark marker, one idea per card. Participants are asked to be non-evaluative.

An interesting variation of this is Loud Brainwriting where each person shouts out the idea he or she is recording. Shouting can stimulate creativity.

Another variation of this is to have everyone write an absurd, bizarre, or exotic idea on a card, then exchange cards and write a new idea based on what appears on the card. Participants are asked to write down the first idea that comes to mind when looking at each new card. After twenty minutes, the cards are placed on tables or pinned to a wall so people can see them.

Clustering Brainwriting. I learned this procedure from Corey Ericson at DuPont, and it uses automatic writing.

You begin with a nucleus-word. This is the problem around which you wish to do some creative thinking. Write the nucleus-word in the center of a piece of paper or flip-chart paper. Now write whatever comes to mind in a cluster around the core word. Do not stop to think about what you are writing. Don't seek connections. You really want random thoughts in the early stages. Go off on wild tangents. Look for different perspectives. And be non-evaluative.

If one of the clouds of thoughts seems interesting, cluster around it for as long as you can be spontaneous. Then return to the original nucleus-word and cluster around it again.

Cluster as long as ideas flow freely. When you run out, let it sit for a time. Then return to the cluster and add new words.

Now study the cluster of words you have created. Non-evaluatively list ideas you might want to try.

Connect word clusters to give new, creative, synergistic approaches to the problem on which you are working.

Show the cluster to someone else to trigger new ideas.

Set a quota for a minimum number of usable ideas. To settle for less than five new ideas is to accept the obvious, the quick fix.

To force combinations between unrelated concepts, use two or more nucleus-words at opposite ends of the same paper. This will force a combination or create a usable metaphor between these concepts.

Brainwriting Circle. I modified clustering in the following way:

I write a word or phrase that captures the spirit of a problem in a small circle in the center of a blank sheet of paper. The size of the paper can vary from 8 ½" x 11" on a writing pad to large flip-chart paper on an easel.

I start a process of progressive free association by writing words close to the circle that remind me of or are associated with the concept within the circle. I use non-evaluative listing and automatic writing.

When there is no more room left next to the circle, I move outward a bit and start writing a new circular layer of words or phrases. I continue until the page is filled with concentric circles of words and phrases triggered by free association with the original word or phrase or with any of the words and phrases that are written on the paper.

I use linear and non-linear creativity throughout. I allow myself to go off on tangents. What I write does not have to make sense or be connected in any way.

When I'm done, I make connections and remote associations by circling and drawing lines between words or phrases that define patterns of new thought and ideas that seem useful in themselves or as triggers to new ideas.

When you try this procedure, be patient. Allow this process to work. It sometimes seems fragile to me, shattering into a useless jumble unless I carefully nurture it by not forcing the words and phrases to make sense too soon.

Using Forced Combinations

Forced combinations help new ideas occur by mixing the properties of two or more objects or thoughts together to spark remote associations. Here's how to make forced combinations help you solve problems creatively:

First, non-evaluatively list the characteristics, associations, reminders, properties, or whatever, of the stimulus trigger-idea. Then write your how-to problem statement. Next, non-evaluatively list the ideas from the forced combinations between your problem and the characteristics, associations, etc., of your stimulus trigger-idea.

The **stimulus trigger-idea** can come from a variety of sources. For example, metaphors can be used to open your mind to new possibilities and new mind funnels you probably would not have thought of otherwise. Here's how this can be done.

Study an object, situation, picture, or thought, very carefully. Non-evaluatively list specific characteristics or properties, such as color, shape, texture, odor, feel, sound, taste, or composition. Choose one property or characteristic, then non-evaluatively list what that property or characteristic reminds you of. For example, a white page in a book is white like snow, smooth like silk, flat like a table top, etc. Then, to use these metaphors to help solve a problem, non-evaluatively list the characteristics, nuances, impressions, etc., of your metaphor. Then force combinations between these metaphors and your how-to problem statement. Select, combine, change, add to, slice, and develop an idea to help solve your problem. You also improve your idea by non-evaluatively listing, in turn, what you like and can use in your idea; what's deficient and needs improving; and ways you can overcome deficiencies.

Analogies can also be used as trigger-stimuli. Choose a culture, civilization, profession, country, ethnic group, organization, animal, or plant. Write the properties of the different culture, civilization, or what have you. Then write down your how-to problem statement. Next, non-evaluatively list the ideas from the forced combinations between the properties and your how-to problem statement.

Pictures are also trigger-stimuli. Take a picture and non-evaluatively list all visual elements in it. Force combinations between specific visual elements and specific elements of the problem you are faced with. Make remote associations that help develop sensible solutions to solve the problem.

We discussed bizarre ideas earlier. They, too, can be used to trigger ideas. For example, in the **Improve Bizarre Ideas Game,** a group is divided into creativity teams. Each team has four minutes to generate the most bizarre, absurd idea to solve a problem. This idea is then passed to another creativity team, which now has four minutes to use this idea as a trigger to spark a better idea. If it does so, it gets one point. If it doesn't, the other team gets a point. And as the game goes on, new ideas are created.

Similar to this is the **Weird-to-Workable Idea Approach.** Here, a recorder divides flip-chart paper into quarters with a magic marker. A creativity team writes a "weird idea" to solve the problem in the first quadrant. The paper passes to another team.

In the second round, the other creativity team uses the "weird idea" to trigger a "better idea" and writes it in the second quadrant. The flip-chart paper is then passed on.

In the third round, the other creativity team uses the "better idea" to trigger a "practical idea" and writes it in the third quadrant.

In the last step, the last group uses the "practical idea" to trigger a "workable idea" and writes it in the fourth quadrant.

In general, the more bizarre or weird the first idea is, the more likely it is that the workable idea will be different, original, and creative.

Another forced combination procedure is **Random Word Trigger-Stimuli,** which combines nonrelevant mind funnels with a problem statement to trigger remote associations. To practice it, use one of the words in the next paragraph and force combinations between it and a problem statement to generate new problem statements and new ideas:

Bears, television, cup and saucer, pea pods, mountains, baseball, bamboo, car, Idaho, clock, telephone, tennis ball, sofa, waterfalls, skiing, dancing, football, Ohio, car, book, house, radio, museum, wine, pencil, watermelon, town, countryside, pen, lamp, cooking, electricity, outer space, pole vault, sculpture, fishing, candle, rock, Kansas, cows, sewing, automobile, religion, laser beam, dice, magic, winter, NYC, meditation, children, rock and roll, astronomy, movies, watch, money, friend, school, mountain, laughter, flying, ocean, key, street, store, knife, universe, home, boxing, horses, Orlando, painting, love.

Here's another version of the random word trigger. Write down a page number and another number chosen at random. Choose a book or dictionary. Turn to the page you listed and count words up to the number you listed. Force combinations between the next word and your problem statement. Generate new problem statements and new ideas.

Consider, too, the use of quotations as trigger-stimuli. Force combinations using your favorite quotes. Begin by non-evaluatively listing ten to twenty famous quotations. From these, choose one quotation that seems particularly alive to you. Or choose one that is impactful or seems catchy or is funny. Now write the quotation down. Next, non-evaluatively list its characteristics, properties, impressions, or what have you. Next, write your how-to problem statement. Force combinations between the characteristics of your quotation and your problem statement, and non-evaluatively list ideas. Select, combine, change, add to, and develop the ideas in order to solve your problem. To improve on an idea, non-evaluatively list what you like and can use. Also, non-evaluatively list what is deficient and needs improving. Convert these into how-to problem statements. Finally, non-evaluatively list ways to improve your idea by solving the problem statement. This process should be repeated as often as necessary.

Idea Grid, also called "morphological analysis," is a very systematic procedure to search out new perspectives and make sure no idea is overlooked. A grid is formed by filling in the top row and side row with categories relating to the main problem. Then forced combinations are made between categories to generate new ideas in each box. Let's assume, for example, that the purpose of the Idea Grid is to improve Creativity Procedures at work. Then the boxes at the top of the grid might be: to increase quality of ideas, to increase quantity of ideas, to help improve new ideas, to increase acceptance and development of ideas, to improve implementation of ideas, to improve screening, evaluation, and selection of ideas. The boxes on the left might be: in meetings, in yourself, in subordinates, in peers, in your work group.

Free Word Association Imagery is a procedure that generates relatively few ideas, but the novelty and uniqueness of the ideas make it very worthwhile. Here's how this procedure works.

Five to six people plus a recorder participate. In the first step, the recorder intuitively selects a dynamic word from the chosen problem statement. Next, people are asked to forget about the problem. Instead, attention is focused on the chosen word. Each person gives a one-word free association beginning with the chosen word and each word thereafter.

The recorder then intuitively picks one of the words. People close their eyes and spend a few minutes forming an image around the chosen word. People describe their images, which are non-evaluatively listed on flip-chart paper.

People then force exotic or bizarre combinations between any of the images and the problem statement. The associations should be impractical, absurd, outrageous.

In the final step, people use the bizarre image associations to trigger practical ideas. These are non-evaluatively listed on flip-chart paper and developed into a trigger-proposal and a potential, sensible, workable solution for the original problem statement.

Combining Teams is a procedure best used with an advanced creativity team. Three groups of five to six people are formed, and one group is designated logical thinkers, one group creative thinkers, and the third is the combining team. The logical and creative groups are given a problem statement. The combining team is idle.

The creative and logical groups generate ideas to solve the problem using non-evaluative listing and idea card brainwriting, with about twenty or thirty minutes for each procedure. The logical group is told to avoid creativity and concentrate only on logical solutions that make sense. The creative group is told that no logical solutions are permitted and all ideas must be bizarre.

The combination-team is given the lists of ideas and asked to force combinations between the ideas of the two groups to develop new, creative, workable solutions.

A variation of this approach is to use only the first two groups, ask them to force combinations between each other's ideas in mixed Buzz Groups.

Future Fantasy

In this category of Creativity Procedures, future expectations are combined with current realities using procedures like the following:

Future Pretend Year. To do this, you first write your how-to problem statement. Now fantasize. Assume it is the future. The problem is solved. All ideas have been successfully implemented. List each person both within and outside your work group who has been positively affected by the success. Now list all those who have been negatively affected. List the resource people who are helping. Fantasize and include experts from the past and present in your company and from other companies and organizations. Next, list other living, historical, or mythological experts or heroes whom you would like to be helping. Add to your list writers, scientists, businesspeople, etc. Now, for each person listed, non-evaluatively list specifically what each is uniquely doing in the future to help implement the successful solution to your problem. Start each item with the name of the person.

Finally, use each activity listed as a trigger-idea to spark new ideas to solve your problem as it exists today. Force combinations between these trigger-ideas and your problem statement.

Future-Present Word Combination. This is a technique that can be used after "Future Pretend Year."

Begin by non-evaluatively listing five to ten "future core words"—that is, adjectives and adverbs that capture the intent or feeling of what you want in your final solution. Choose three of these.

Describe your perception of your problem. Non-evaluatively list what you have tried, selecting the most impactful, and non-evaluatively list why each failed. Next, write your how-to problem statement.

The next step is to non-evaluatively list five to ten "present core words"—that is, adjectives and adverbs that capture your impressions and feelings about the present problem. These are often the opposites of the "future core words" in the first step. Choose three.

Next, make a grid and combine each of your "future core words" with each of the three "present core words" (e.g., hot-cold). In each combination, make the first word an adjective and the second word a noun (e.g., hot-coldness or cold-hotness). These are bridge combinations.

Then, choose the bridge combination that best captures the present-future situation (e.g., hot-coldness).

Now, choose a metaphor to help solve your problem creatively. Use one that is a working example of your chosen bridge combination. For example, an air conditioner is a bridging-image of hot-coldness. Non-evaluatively list the properties, characteristics, and attributes of your metaphor, and force combinations with your bridge combination stated as a how-to problem statement. Now, non-evaluatively list ideas. Pick the most interesting, bizarre, or impractical trigger-idea. Now improve your trigger idea by practicing Like-Improve Analysis on the chosen idea (see Chapter 7).

Special Sequences

Often, a sequence of Creativity Procedures is necessary to generate new ideas. One sequence I like to use during a problem-solving creativity meeting consists of Non-evaluative Listing, Improve Bizarre Ideas Game, Weird-to-Workable Idea Game, Idea Gallery Brainwriting, Free Word Association Imagery, and Idea Card Brainwriting.

Why combine a variety of Creativity Procedures? I find a sequence like this is helpful to teach participants, in turn, to be non-evaluative (Non-evaluative Listing), to value and use bizarre ideas to trigger better ideas (Improve Bizarre Ideas Game and the Weird-to-Workable Idea Approach), to generate bizarre ideas and force-fit them to the problem (Free Word Association Imagery), and to quietly reflect and record ideas alone as individuals (Idea Gallery and Idea Card Brainwriting). And best of all, as all this learning takes place, many hundreds of ideas are generated to solve the problem creatively.

The Idea Improvement Checklist

Once you have selected an idea, you'll want to improve on it as much as you can. To do this, you may want to use the Like-Improve Analysis described in Chapter 7. Also useful at this stage is the idea checklist developed by A. F. Osborn (1963), the originator of brainstorming. The checklist is a series of questions designed to help you improve on your ideas by expanding how you see your problem. Look at your problem statement and ideas, and ask yourself the following:

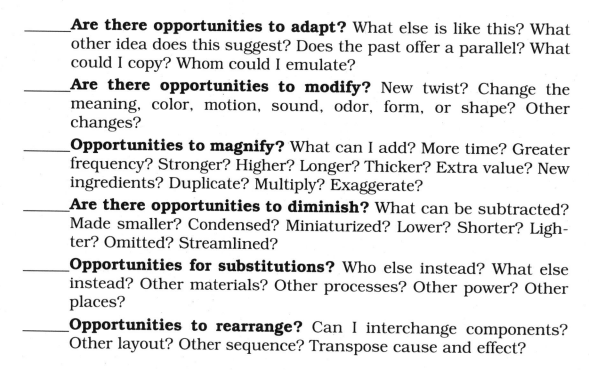

_____**Are there opportunities to adapt?** What else is like this? What other idea does this suggest? Does the past offer a parallel? What could I copy? Whom could I emulate?

_____**Are there opportunities to modify?** New twist? Change the meaning, color, motion, sound, odor, form, or shape? Other changes?

_____**Opportunities to magnify?** What can I add? More time? Greater frequency? Stronger? Higher? Longer? Thicker? Extra value? New ingredients? Duplicate? Multiply? Exaggerate?

_____**Are there opportunities to diminish?** What can be subtracted? Made smaller? Condensed? Miniaturized? Lower? Shorter? Lighter? Omitted? Streamlined?

_____**Opportunities for substitutions?** Who else instead? What else instead? Other materials? Other processes? Other power? Other places?

_____**Opportunities to rearrange?** Can I interchange components? Other layout? Other sequence? Transpose cause and effect?

_____**Are there opportunities to reverse?** Transpose positive and negative? How about opposites? Turn it backward? Turn it upside down? Reverse roles? Turn tables? Turn the other cheek?

_____Finally, **are there opportunities to combine?** How about a blend, an alloy, an assortment, an ensemble? Combine units? Combine purposes? Combine ideas?

The main purpose of the checklist is to force-fit further combinations between the idea and problem statement to improve on-the-job creativity.

Identifying Criteria to Choose Ideas

Choose criteria carefully. There is little point in going through these Creativity Procedures and not selecting the best idea among the good ones. Yet that is often what happens. To help you in making your choice, you may want to consider the following criteria:

- Ease of testing and startup;
- Costs. Consider both tangible costs (like materials, equipment, space, and personnel) and intangible costs (like opinions, attitudes, feelings, and aesthetics);
- Difficulties of implementation;
- Technical feasibility. Consider whether the idea is compatible with the work group. Also, consider its marketability;
- Effect on overall goals;
- Individuals and groups affected;
- Moral and legal implications;
- New problems caused;
- Consequences of both success and failure;
- Timeliness;
- Benefits to you, your team, and your company;
- Your gut feelings.

In the next chapter, we'll look further into ways to combine ideas into workable solutions—the third key step in creative problem solving.

Chapter 9

Combining Ideas into Workable Solutions: The Third Key Creative Step

After you've generated ideas, how do you sort and categorize them? One useful approach is the *Idea Board.*

The Idea Board

Simply put, an Idea Board is a large bulletin board covered with ideas written on index cards (one idea per card), arranged in themes and categories. The cards should be easily readable and easy to move around on the board.

The Idea Board can be used in conjunction with Brainwriting or it can be used to display stages and steps in a specific planning process.

The cards can be organized in vertical columns, and different-colored cards can be used for various purposes. The headings and groupings should be reviewed by the work group periodically. For example, do all the cards in a given category belong there? Are there enough categories? Used properly, the idea board will be a useful way to sort and combine new ideas.

Forced Withdrawal and Trigger-Proposals

Often you will find yourself using unstated criteria to select ideas or rejecting ideas you think others would laugh at. This hampers a truly creative and sensible proposal.

Free up your creative juices with a bit of fantasy I call *Forced Withdrawal,* in which you select ideas to solve a problem related to, but quite distant from, your actual problem. This allows you to use and combine ideas you might otherwise prematurely reject.

Suppose you're trying to solve the problem of how to stimulate creativity in your work group. Your "forced withdrawal" would be to prepare a creative proposal to stimulate creativity in a "new company." Create an imaginary company. Then non-evaluatively list all your ideas about what might go into a proposal on index cards. Let the creative juices flow freely. Take those ideas and combine and modify them in any way that makes sense to you. If necessary, list new ideas on additional index cards. Then sort the cards and evaluate the ideas. Put them in whatever sequence you want and write out a one-page *Trigger-Proposal.*

Now do the same, only this time with the real problem for which you need a real solution. Follow the same steps and finish with a sensible, workable proposal.

You can also use your index cards to help prepare reports for your work group.

The reason for "forced withdrawals" is that they put distance between you and the problem. You can generate new ideas free of the constraints of old mind funnels and perspectives. These can be especially crippling if you are too close to the problem.

The Role of Structure in Creativity

By now you must be wondering why there is so much structure in the process of being creative. Isn't it usually a helter-skelter free-for-all? Yes—and no. Actually, creativity works best for many people within specific structures and special disciplines. The intense focus and tuning out of extraneous stimuli necessary for creativity requires structure and enforced discipline. This is not to box the creative person in, but rather to keep out unwanted distractions.

The special conditions vary with the person and the team. The important point is to be deliberate in setting up the structure and then sticking to it. You must be relentless in protecting it from breaking down by keeping distractions and interruptions from interfering with the creative process. Above all, be assertive and say "No" to the creative spoilers around you.

Chapter 10

Creativity Procedures to Use in Regular Meetings

You'll want to apply all the Creativity Procedures described in this book in your regular meetings. To do this, you first have to understand what spoils creativity during meetings.

Creativity Spoilers

Experts have identified the following as detrimental to the productivity of problem-solving sessions.

- Members judge ideas prematurely;
- Minimal sharing of ideas occurs;
- Highly vocal people dominate;
- People are overwhelmed by experts or high-ranking superiors;
- People lack training in Creativity Procedures;
- People are not told that creativity is wanted;
- People are not interested and involved;
- People are fixed on achieving the mission, not on generating new ideas;
- People conceal emotions, and this inhibits spontaneity;
- People use win-lose methods, like "majority rules."
- People funnel problems prematurely, practicing the quick fix;
- People do not solve problems in structured ways;
- People are confused about goals and purposes;
- People use analytical and logical thinking all the time;
- The leader encourages ideas most similar to his or her own preconceived notions through verbal and nonverbal feedback.

Which of these describe your meetings?

Increasing Meeting Creativity

To turn the situation around—to increase the creativity in your meet-ings—you need to do the following more often:

- Use Creativity Procedures to define problems and generate myriad ideas;
- Select ideas innovatively;
- Generate trigger-proposals creatively;
- Develop workable solutions logically;
- Select proposals systematically;
- Postpone evaluation and defer judgment of new ideas;
- Establish a quota for many really different ideas before selection;
- When hearing new ideas, use I.P.N.C., Yes, if..., and I.I.A;
- State what you like about the idea first;
- Use effective team interaction procedures: make decisions by consensus, record on flip charts so all can see, allow leadership roles to distribute naturally, circulate the agenda beforehand and action plans afterward, rotate the chair of the meeting, and discuss and evaluate interactions at frequent intervals, especially discuss-ing what spoils creativity and productivity. You may want to study Table 1 to better understand the chairperson's role in helping stimulate creativity.

Getting Started

If you suspect that your work group does not look forward to problem-solving creativity meetings, you may want to address the situation directly at the meeting. At the next session, ask your work group members to reverse the problem statement "how to stimulate creativity during our meetings" into "how to spoil creativity during our meetings." Then dereverse each creativity spoiler (as described in Chapter 7, "Reverse Assumptions") by writing "how to" in front of each idea and creatively smoothing out the sentence into a sensible problem statement.

For example, you could dereverse the creativity spoiler "have domi-neering people present" into "how to be creative with domineering people present" or into "how to keep domineering people out."

Another creativity spoiler, "holding meetings at 4:45 on Friday" could be dereversed into "how to be creative in a meeting held at 4:45 on Friday" or "how to prevent a meeting being called at this time."

Using this procedure, you will shortly have a lot of problem state-ments focusing on the specific needs of the group. The group can then break up into Buzz Groups and non-evaluatively list solutions to the problem statements that impact the most on work group meetings.

As you put into practice the ideas from the session, the creativity of your regular meetings will improve. In the next chapter, we will look at ways you can increase the creativity of the special meetings and retreats you hold.

Table 1. CHAIR MEETINGS TO HELP CREATIVITY[*]

Please check those you want to improve.

Suggested Options	*Reasons*
___ 1. Do not compete with your work group in generating viable ideas. You should support and build on the ideas of others.	1. Leaders are apt to favor their own ideas. This tends to discourage members of the work group from participating.
___ 2. Listen non-evaluatively. Your job is to create an atmosphere in which all ideas are considered.	2. Listening non-evaluatively will model an important way to encourage everyone to participate.
___ 3. Do not permit anyone to be put on the defensive. Find value in all points of view. Start with what you like about what you heard.	3. This approach encourages everyone to contribute and help new ideas.
___ 4. Get people to talk about the positives of an idea before the negatives. Do not kill an idea; just put it aside.	4. This approach encourages everyone to contribute and help new ideas.
___ 5. Keep the energy level high.	5. Your interest and alertness can help your work group.
___ 6. Use every member of your work group. Verbose members need to be talked to privately. Quiet persons need to be helped.	6. Everyone has unique mind funnels, valuable ideas, and information that increase the quality of the work group's output.
___ 7. Tape your meetings and ask persons with poor behavior to listen to the tape.	7. This can help them to change their behavior.
___ 8. Rotate the responsibility for chairing the meeting.	8. Being a follower and leader can lead to commitment and participation.
___ 9. Do not damage egos or self-images.	9. This will encourage everyone to share and lead to greater levels of participation.
___10. Defer judgment during idea generation and avoid early commitment to an idea.	10. The leader has great power to sway members. This does not always result in choosing and developing the best idea

---

*Adapted from *The Practice of Creativity* by George M. Prince. Copyright © 1970 by George M. Prince. Reprinted by permission of HarperCollins Publishers.

Chapter 11

Special Creativity Procedures for Special Creativity Teams

Special creativity teams are composed of people in your work group who are trained in diverse Creativity Procedures and who can generate alternative problem statements and numerous ideas for you to consider. You provide the starting problem statement and based on your own criteria, you choose the final problem statement(s) the special creativity team will use as the basis for generating ideas.

How It Works

First, a leader of the special creativity team is chosen to act as a servant of the team, making the arrangements for the meeting and to act as the recorder during the session. The team leader will also help you clarify the problem you will present to the special creativity team.

Second, the five to eight members of the special creativity team are chosen. They provide the diverse mind funnels and different perspectives, as well as the creative energy to generate endless problem statements and new ideas. Their only reward is the intrinsic fun of creativity and in helping others to solve problems.

Finally: There is the problem-presenter with the appropriate commitment to solve the problem. You, as problem-presenter, must present the problem clearly to the special creativity team, and time should be spent with the team leader ahead of the creativity meeting to make sure this occurs. You should be an expert able to present the necessary information.

You should know when to be non-evaluative and temporarily suspend judgment so the process can work.

Creativity Team Sessions

The sequence and time allotted for a session of a special creativity team will vary with the importance of the problem. Sometimes a sixty-minute meeting mimicking a Buzz Group session is sufficient. Sometimes an entire day, or more, using many procedures for defining problems and generating ideas, is necessary.

Here's a sequence of Creativity Procedures I find useful for a special creativity team:

1. The problem-presenter presents the problem;
2. The recorder non-evaluatively lists the how-to problem statements suggested by the creativity team, about ten to twenty;
3. The problem-presenter chooses the problem statement for the creativity team to work on;
4. The recorder non-evaluatively lists thirty to fifty ideas suggested by the creativity team;
5. The recorder non-evaluatively lists five to fifteen bizarre trigger-ideas suggested by the creativity team;
6. The creativity team combines and improves the most bizarre ideas;
7. Each member of the creativity team then sits quietly writing ideas using idea cards;
8. All the sheets, flip-chart papers, and cards are given to the problem-presenter;
9. The creativity team then applies Like-Improve Analysis to the functioning of the team and non-evaluatively lists what each person liked and what each wants improved to make the special creativity team even more effective in the future.

Role of the Problem-Presenter

It is important that the team leader play the appropriate servant and advisor roles and that you, as problem-presenter, present a low profile, not act defensively, not put any idea down ("we thought of that one" or "we tried that one"), and thank everyone at the end for the excellent ideas generated.

When asked if any of the ideas seem useful, the answer should be an enthusiastic "Yes." It's an important reward for the special creativity team.

Some True Stories

Shortly after I presented a creativity workshop at an R&D unit of a Fortune 500 company, I received a call from one of the managers who asked if I remembered a participant.

"He's an excellent engineer but never listened to subordinates' ideas. After your workshop, he started conducting creativity meetings with them using the procedures he learned in your workshop. Yesterday he and one of his subordinates showed me an idea the subordinate had suggested and it's terrific. Very simple and it should be easy to implement. We are going to see people about marketing it next week."

Another time, I presented a one-day creativity workshop for a director of information systems of a Fortune 500 company and thirty-three of his managers and computer analysts. In the afternoon, I formed six groups of special creativity teams who worked on a problem presented by their director.

They helped define the problem by suggesting over fifty how-to problem statements. He chose six of these.

Based on these, the groups generated hundreds of ideas using Non-evaluative Listing, Improve Bizarre Ideas Game, Idea Gallery, and Idea Card.

A really good time was had by all, and the problem seemed on the way toward solution. Last I heard they were discussing the best way to sort and select ideas.

Writing Up Your Problem

For these kinds of results, as problem-presenter, you have to be sure you have identified the right problem. To help you, here is a list of questions you should ask yourself:

- What would be some indicators of success?

- What resources are available to help resolve the problem?

- What obstacles must be overcome?

- What is the deadline?

Now, in two to four sentences, write a balanced, broad-brush overview of your problem. As part of this, list what you might lose if the problem isn't solved. Also, list what you will gain if the problem is solved. List, too, the approaches and solutions you have already tried and why each of these has failed. Finally, list the benefits of the status quo and the advantages of doing nothing.

From this analysis, you should be able to develop about a dozen how-to statements. Non-evaluatively list these and choose two to four to work on. Finally, summarize your problem in one how-to statement.

Chapter 12

Putting It Together in a Creativity Meeting

In the previous chapters, we have looked at a variety of Creativity Procedures as well as described how to use special creativity teams. Using the six-step problem-solving process described in Chapter 6, let's see how these Creativity Procedures would be used in a real problem-solving creativity meeting.

Step 1. Define problems creatively. (See Chapter 7). To do this:

- List dozens of problem statements;
- Try to identify the problem's essence;
- Target analogies and metaphors based on the problem's essence;
- Conduct the like-improve analysis;
- Use the guided fresh eye approach;
- Reverse and dereverse;
- Reverse assumptions;
- Practice word substitutions;
- Ask why, who, what, where, and when; then why, again;
- Identify needs, obstacles, and constraints;
- Identify weaknesses of quick-fix solutions.

Step 2. Identify criteria for selecting the best problem statements from among many.

Step 3. Choose the final problem statement(s).

Step 4. Generate ideas abundantly. For those procedures you want to use, see Chapter 8. Consider:

- Brainstorming
- Buzz Groups
- Idea Gallery Brainwriting
- Idea Card Brainwriting
- Clustering Brainwriting
- Brainwriting Circle

- Forced Combinations and Stimulus Trigger-Ideas; Metaphors; Analogies; Pictures

- Random Word Trigger Stimuli; Quotations

- Idea Grid

- Improve Bizarre Ideas Game

- Weird-to-Workable Idea Approach

- Free Word Association Imagery

- Combining Teams

- Future Fantasy

- Future Pretend Year

- Future-Present Word Combination

- Like-Improve Analysis

Step 5. Identify the criteria for choosing ideas.

Step 6. Combine ideas into trigger-ideas and sensible, workable solutions. (See chapter 9.) Consider:

- Creative Trigger-Proposals

- Idea Board

- Forced Withdrawal

- Return to Reality

Set a quota during the problem-solving creativity meetings of 50 to 150 problem statements, 100 to 300 ideas, and three to six trigger-proposals before generating the final workable solution.

Chapter 13

"The Biggest Help to My Creativity at Work is...When My Boss Leaves Town"

Do you want to motivate people to be creative (and not by leaving town)? Research has shown that people turn out more creative work and find more creative solutions to problems if they are intrinsically motivated. In other words, they need to focus their attention on their daily enjoyment, the challenges of the work, the joy of problem solving, and their total immersion in the process.

If you want people to solve problems more creatively, don't distract them from these intrinsic motivators. Otherwise, you will spoil their creativity. Focus their attention (and yours, too) on their day-to-day enjoyment of their work, and give them as many choices as you can in how to do the job. Invest in high job stability so that your people will engage in risk taking.

I am told of one team leader who would ask his people every day, "Are you having fun?" He would ask to share the fun with those who said yes and would help those who said no to have fun.

Extrinsic rewards—salary increases, promotions, honors—are necessary, but they decrease the likelihood that the same activity will be performed as well in the absence of a reward. They remind the worker that he or she is engaged in work rather than play, and they spoil creativity. Intrinsic rewards—enjoyment, challenge, self-satisfaction—increase interest in the job itself and actually enhance performance and creativity.

I often ask my workshop participants to fill out a questionnaire. One statement I ask them to complete is "When I am creating, I feel...." Almost everyone uses words like excited, fulfilled, enthusiastic, stimulated, happy, delighted, and fun. Fewer than 3 percent list negative feelings about creativity.

We all need salary increases and promotions and bonuses but see if the creativity level doesn't rise if you start focusing on the daily enjoyment of work.

Here are some other statements on my questionnaire. You can jot down how you would complete each:

"The biggest help to my creativity at work is...."

"The biggest obstacle to my creativity at work is...."

"I need the following from my job environment to be more creative...."

Many people (nearly half) respond to the first statement with, "interaction with other people." Only 30 percent mentioned being alone and having uninterrupted time as key aids. We can gather from this that you can improve creativity in your workplace by encouraging more frequent and effective discussions among your team members.

What blocks on-the-job creativity? The responses to this are more vague. Some people note such personal problems as newness to the job, lack of creative skills, and so forth. Other responses include lack of time, lack of freedom, negative criticism, distractions, low acceptance of new ideas, and red tape. The good news here is that most of these problems can be corrected if you are willing to make the effort.

Respondents to the third statement list the following as key items necessary for increased creativity: more freedom and time, less red tape and routing, better resources, and increased respect. You need to ask your people what they need to be creative, and what spoils on-the-job creativity. Create your own questionnaire.

Individualized Motivating Catalysts

Some people work better when listening to music; others need absolute quiet. But when customized work environments exceed the level of tolerable nonconformity, the person may have to change his or her behavior, which can result in less creativity.

One executive I know would go to work on weekends so that he could work alone in his underwear—this was when he felt most creative, probably a leftover from his student days. Is this too bizarre? Perhaps, but my hunch is that a lot of people have similar borderline behaviors that trigger their creativity. I call them *motivating catalysts,* and they are not unknown among famous figures. Wagner composed his best work while stroking velvet. Emile Zola worked best in artificial light and would pull his shades down during the day to work. Picasso could not paint well unless someone else was in the room with him.

Of course, some behavior is not feasible at work—but easing up on conformity might loosen people enough to let them be more creative. Perhaps some small changes will lead to great increases in on-the-job creativity.

Situational Creativity Theory

People with high creative ability do not always have highly creative outputs. Specific job conditions will determine the results. Thus, someone may be very creative and still have relatively non-creative outputs, depending on the particular work situation.

Workshops may help in the development of personal skills to resist a creativity-spoiling job environment and to immunize people against creativity spoilers. This includes workshops in selling ideas, team-excellence skills, and time management. Still, the job environment and its climate need to be in line to help creative outcomes. Otherwise, the motivation for on-the-job creativity declines and dies.

In addition, not being able to communicate new ideas to others spoils motivation for on-the-job creativity. This happens mainly in older projects with well-developed ideas, rather than in new projects. Thus, the creative person helps newly formed units but hurts and may be hurt at later stages. Intrinsic motivation is overwhelmed. This is because a highly coordinated, goal-oriented work group strives to achieve its mission and spoils on-the-job creativity with its lack of flexibility.

The outcome for a creative person in a non-flexible environment can be disappointment, dejection, and resentment. Intrinsic motivation and on-the-job creativity are spoiled. Choices for the creative person are to leave the job or cut down on creative outcomes. Often intrinsic motivation disappears, and the creative person retires on the job, becoming what I call a weekend creative. By channeling creative energies into weekend pursuits, the creative person does poorer on the job than less creative colleagues. This outcome is not beneficial to the work group or the organization. This phenomenon needs to be creatively addressed in a way that recaptures these weekend energies and channels them into on-the-job creativity. Figure 1 illustrates the creativity-security dilemma.

THE CREATIVITY-SECURITY DILEMMA

Companies want people with creative ability to produce creative outputs. Unfortunately there is a creativity-security dilemma that can create inflexibility. As shown below, risky new ideas can threaten the security of colleagues. This leads to subtle or overt negative feedback to the idea person, whose sense of job security is now jeopardized. Intrinsic motivation for on-the-job creativity declines. The result is either less creativity or worsening relations between the idea person and colleagues, or the idea person leaves or retires on the job and becomes a weekend creative. It operates this way:

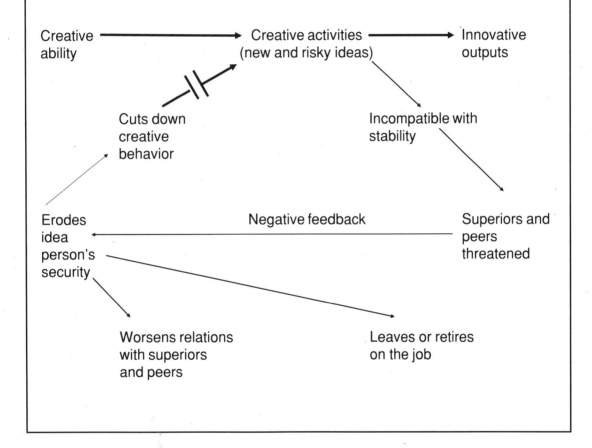

Figure 1. THE CREATIVITY-SECURITY DILEMMA

Chapter 14

Team Building for On-the-Job Creativity

When you are the team leader, how do you lead your work group? Are you a "star with helpers" or a "first among equals"?

Rather than trying to make a quick change, it is best for you to realize that flexibility is the best approach. Sometimes it's better to be a "star" and sometimes it's best to be a "first." And sometimes, it's best to combine both approaches.

If you want to be more adept as a first among equals, here's a simple team-building approach:

Set aside time at the end of each meeting to discuss the quality of the meeting interaction and the quality of the meeting results. Watch for those who are too glib or too enthusiastic.

Focus on what went well and also on what needs improvement. Who dominated? Who said nothing? What helped the discussion? What hindered it? If there is a problem, and if you sense that you are part of the problem, ask for ways you can become part of the solution. Perhaps a rotating chair might be better than having the same person serve as chair at every meeting.

Next, ask everyone to answer with a rating (on a one-to-ten scale) the following: To what extent was participation equally balanced among members? To what extent were thoughts and opinions solicited by the team? How much do you feel you influenced the meeting? How much did others influence the final outcome? Also ask to what extent the team found the meeting creative.

Ask everyone to list what behaviors they found most helpful to the team effort and what spoiled creativity.

Ask for a one-sentence comment on each of these issues from everyone and give a written summary at the next meeting.

Then, you should use a questionnaire on team excellence to gather important information on how your work group sees itself and how it sees you in terms of its effectiveness. (See the appendices for samples.)

Your Leadership Style

Research has shown that most leader interactions at work fall into two basic types: *task behaviors* (directive one-way communications explaining what each person is to do and how) and *supportive behaviors* (which involve and encourage two-way communication, non-evaluative listening and encouragement). How you use these interactions defines your leadership style.

The four basic leadership styles are as follows:

Directive: telling, asserting, and modeling

Participative: coaching, negotiating, collaborating

Catalytic: encouraging, facilitating, consulting

Non-Directive: delegating

When choosing leadership interactions, think of the ability of a given person to work independently of you. If the person is self-motivated and has high ability and strong skills, a directive style will not do.

Adjust Your Style

Why not make your leadership style work for you? It may be difficult, but it is also a good way to make yourself more flexible. You can add one or two skills at a time so you can become more flexible. Or you might want to get specific training.

Leaders who want to find out what spoils creativity for excellence and renewal need to ask their teams for advice and feedback. Freedom may be the most common request. True, freedom is a key component of creativity. But complete freedom seems less effective than moderate freedom coupled with supportive consultations.

In addition, many leaders have habits that interfere with the on-the-job creativity of their teams. Perhaps you don't expect your people to be creative. Or perhaps you want quick results all the time. Maybe you fall into the pattern of quick negative criticism.

Many leaders fail to realize that their own behavior can have such an impact on their teams. They must form the habit of setting direction, giving clear ideas of what should be accomplished, and letting teams do their work as they see fit.

Chapter 15

Helping Creativity Through Self-Direction

Self-directed activity in which intrinsic motivation is high has been shown to help creativity. One way to maximize the performance of your work group is to create an atmosphere of responsible self-direction—"responsible" because the team recognizes and respects organizational goals; "self-direction" because people are motivated to do their job independently and well.

Cycle Your Leadership Interaction Behaviors

To help your team members become more self-directed and creative, cycle your leadership interactions from directive to nondirective. Your behavior should change as people get better at their respective jobs. If you use only the participative style, people in your team will probably not become as self-directed and motivated as they could. The independence generated by the non-directive style and the encouragement generated by the catalytic style are sometimes necessary for creativity.

Research shows that team excellence training can be beneficial and that teams trained in procedures for achieving true consensus often produce creative solutions of higher quality. Cohesiveness and commitment are higher as well.

Disagreements should be negotiated as soon as possible to keep creativity levels high. Again, if there is too much discord, specific training might be in order.

Participative goal setting is another way to encourage your team. Instead of telling your team what your goals are, let each member tell you his or her goals. If you agree, back them to the hilt; if not, negotiate mutually acceptable goals. Also, the use of frequent feedback on performance will help people know their strengths and weaknesses and make them feel more sure of themselves than if they get no feedback.

Again, if certain skills are lacking in your team, provide training for individuals so that they can use their skills and talents wisely.

Chapter 16

The Role of Low and High Conformers

Alert team players can identify two types of team members. *High conformers* prefer to define problems along fairly conventional paths, keeping within team norms. *Low conformers*, on the other hand, ignore boundaries and in fact prefer the bizarre approach to the conventional. They enjoy rocking the boat.

Nearly all work teams are composed of members of both groups. No one, however, is a pure low or high conformer. How can you tell where individuals fit on the scale? As a simple approach, you can examine the basic traits below and circle the ones that apply.

- High conformers tend to be: precise, reliable, efficient, dependable, compliant, sensitive, team-oriented, stable, conventional.

- Low conformers tend to be: undisciplined, easily bored, adamant, impractical, abrasive, undependable, disrespectful of custom.

A team without enough high conformers staggers toward chaos—but a team without enough low conformers staggers toward complacency. The key to remember is that both types are equally creative within their respective styles. Low conformers may appear to be more creative because they take more risks and use more bizarre ideas. But in fact the high conformers can also be very creative.

Bridgers

There is a middle group—*bridgers*—whose moderation can create a cohesive atmosphere within the team. When serving as team leader, you should be a bridger, because you need to be able to communicate with everyone on your team. A leader who is a high conformer may be viewed as too rigid, while a leader who is a low conformer may be considered too scatterbrained and arbitrary.

High conformers think of low conformers as difficult, undependable loners. Low conformers think of high conformers as uptight bureaucrats. Is it any wonder that bridgers are necessary? Actually, the key is not just to have bridgers, but to get the two extreme groups to respect each other and realize that each performs a vital function and that the two extremes can be mutually beneficial.

It is essential for both low and high conformers to understand that there cannot be excellence and renewal within the work group without collaboration between the two extremes.

Leading the Low Conformer

Besides getting low and high conformers to help each other, you will have to understand the low conformer sufficiently to lead him or her.

Most team leaders are skilled at managing the high conformer. After all, high conformers are likely to work well in groups and cooperate with policies and work-group norms. It's the low conformer who requires different approaches.

Since you need low conformers in order to escape routine complacency in your work group, you will have to stretch your leadership style to include behaviors that focus mainly on the catalytic and nondirective styles with a careful sortie, occasionally, into the participative style. There are exceptions to all rules, but low conformers tend to be loners and need special conditions to encourage them to solve the right problems creatively. Leading low conformers requires skill, knowledge, and a special capacity for patience and goodwill.

Chapter 17

Is Training In Creativity Procedures the Answer?

Training in Creativity Procedures is only one part of the total approach that leads to greater effectiveness. Whether you provide training for on-the-job creativity depends on many factors. Ultimately, the final factor is your own good judgment on how you will improve performance within your work group and whether more creativity will provide the solution.

Is your team too complacent? Then you should find ways to stimulate creativity, to keep people from pigeonholing themselves and their ideas.

If everyone is thinking alike—or doing very little thinking—if no one seems to care what anyone is doing; if fewer people ask meaningful questions; if product or service levels have remained constant, then creativity training is probably a good idea.

The previous chapters have pointed out that creativity is within virtually everyone's reach. If you and your work group approach it in a practical, open-minded way, you will get results. Training won't turn anyone on your work group into an Einstein, but it will definitely help people learn procedures to find better quality solutions to problems.

Appendix A

A Dozen Ways to Put Creativity in Your Work Group

1. Discuss and share books and articles on creativity during luncheon discussion groups.

2. Use Creativity Procedures to solve problems more effectively.

3. Provide creativity training for your work group.

4. Bring in guest speakers and creativity consultants now and then.

5. Reward creative accomplishment with more time and resources to enjoy the challenge of being creative again. Foster the enjoyment of intrinsic motivation in your team.

6. Celebrate "Creativity Day" at work now and then. Wear funny hats. Use everyone's creativity to decide what to do that day that would stimulate everyone's creativity.

7. Stop criticizing new ideas so quickly.

8. Revive the pleasure of knowing you are creative and competent.

9. Stop your automatic habitual "No" when confronted with new ideas.

10. Mentally resist the lures of future external rewards and concentrate on immediate intrinsic enjoyment and self-motivation while focusing on creativity.

11. Relentlessly squeeze out new alternative solutions. Set a quota for new ideas.

12. Transform old ideas into new ones. Recombine, magnify, minimize, distort, reverse, add to, subtract from, attribute, reduce, condense, expand, delete, double, digress, drain, manipulate, twist, entwine, titillate, charm, weaken, liquify, fantasize, pray, meditate, commune, daydream, put aside, connect, disconnect, assemble, reassemble, disassemble, take apart, consume.

13. Incubate your ideas often with your shoes off.

14. Use the bizarre trigger-idea to stimulate new and different ideas in your work group.

15. Raise your level of tolerating low conformity for bizarre ideas, clothes, and behaviors in your work group.

16. Do not notice or comment on the fact that there are more than a dozen ideas here. Such quick negative criticism over such a trivial issue spoils motivation for creativity.

Appendix B

The Creativity Leadership
Feedback Questionnaire

If you are a team leader, the people in your work group can provide you with valuable data on how you impact their creativity. Small adjustments in your leadership style can result in a large improvement in your effectiveness, more motivation for them to be creative, and an increase in the creativity of your team.

Your leadership style is the collection of behaviors that you use to influence the people in your work group to accomplish goals. Your real style is what the people in your work group perceive it to be, and that is not always what you think it is.

To determine the real style of the team leader (i.e., to find out how the members of the work group perceive his or her leadership interactions and how he or she impacts their on-the-job creativity) each member of the work group should complete the instrument in this appendix.

Arrange for the answers to be conveyed to the team leader anonymously, to encourage frankness, and in such a way that potentially embarrassing information does not remain a part of the culture of the work group nor deposited in its files.

One way to do this is to give each person in your work group a stamped envelope addressed to an outside consultant or a trusted friend who will compile and deliver the answers to the team leader in a way that will not associate any comments with a specific person. All responses should be kept absolutely confidential and revealed in anonymous summarized form only to the team leader. In addition, the consultant or friend can help plan responses to the feedback.

The team leader should fill out one set on himself or herself and save it to compare with the perceptions of the others in the work group.

How Do You Perceive Your Team Leader's Interactions With You?
(Style I)

Circle the appropriate numbers in columns B, C, and D for each behavior.

A	B		C		D	
Leadership Interactions	How often does your team leader do this?		How well does your team leader do this?		How often is your team leader's interaction appropriate to your work-related needs?*	
			Needs			
	Rarely Often		Improvement Well		Rarely Often	
	1 2 3 4 5		1 2 3 4 5		1 2 3 4 5	
STYLE I						
a) Decides and tells you *what* to do.	1 2 3 4 5		1 2 3 4 5		1 2 3 4 5	
b) Decides and tells you *how* you are to do each task.	1 2 3 4 5		1 2 3 4 5		1 2 3 4 5	
c) Decides and tells you *when* to do each task.	1 2 3 4 5		1 2 3 4 5		1 2 3 4 5	
d) Models and demonstrates *how* each task is to be done.	1 2 3 4 5		1 2 3 4 5		1 2 3 4 5	
e) Decides solutions to disagreements alone.	1 2 3 4 5		1 2 3 4 5		1 2 3 4 5	
TOTAL (Add the numbers that you circled in each column)						

*Your work-related needs might include training, role modeling, coaching, encouragement, feedback on performance, delegation, negotiation, collaboration, teamwork, and listening. You may want to specify which ones you are referring to by circling them here. Add others if appropriate.

How Do You Perceive Your Team Leader's Interaction With You?
(Style II)

Circle the appropriate numbers in columns B, C, and D for each behavior.

A	B					C					D				
Leadership Interactions	How often does your team leader do this?					How well does your team leader do this?					How often is your team leader's interaction appropriate to your work-related needs?*				
	Rarely				Often	Needs Improvement				Well	Rarely				Often
	1	2	3	4	5	1	2	3	4	5	1	2	3	4	5
STYLE II															
a) Solicits and listens to your ideas.	1	2	3	4	5	1	2	3	4	5	1	2	3	4	5
b) Coaches you in your work when needed.	1	2	3	4	5	1	2	3	4	5	1	2	3	4	5
c) Gives frequent, informal feedback on performance.	1	2	3	4	5	1	2	3	4	5	1	2	3	4	5
d) Allows you to participate more and more in planning and decision making.	1	2	3	4	5	1	2	3	4	5	1	2	3	4	5
e) Negotiates disagreements by mutual problem solving.	1	2	3	4	5	1	2	3	4	5	1	2	3	4	5
TOTAL (Add the numbers that you circled in each column.															

---

*Your work-related needs might include training, role modeling, coaching, encouragement, feedback on performance, delegation, negotiation, collaboration, teamwork, and listening. You may want to specify which ones you are referring to by circling them here. Add others if appropriate.

How Do You Perceive Your Team Leader's Interactions With You?
(Style III)

Circle the appropriate numbers in columns B, C, and D for each behavior.

A	B					C					D				
Leadership Interactions	How often does your team leader do this?					How well does your team leader do this?					How often is your team leader's interaction appropriate to your work-related needs?*				
	Rarely				Often	Needs Improvement				Well	Rarely				Often
	1	2	3	4	5	1	2	3	4	5	1	2	3	4	5
STYLE III															
a) Allows you to make decisions and solve problems associated with your specific task.	1	2	3	4	5	1	2	3	4	5	1	2	3	4	5
b) Consults with you on your assignments mainly to provide support and encouragement.	1	2	3	4	5	1	2	3	4	5	1	2	3	4	5
c) Listens and responds non-evaluatively.	1	2	3	4	5	1	2	3	4	5	1	2	3	4	5
d) Encourages independence.	1	2	3	4	5	1	2	3	4	5	1	2	3	4	5
e) Resolves disagreements between you and others in a catalytic, non-evaluative way.	1	2	3	4	5	1	2	3	4	5	1	2	3	4	5
TOTAL (Add the numbers that you circled in each column)															

*Your work-related needs might include training, role modeling, coaching, encouragement, feedback on performance, delegation, negotiation, collaboration, teamwork, and listening. You may want to specify which ones you are referring to by circling them here. Add others if appropriate.

How Do You Perceive Your Team Leader's Interactions With You?
(Style IV)

Circle the appropriate numbers in columns B, C, and D for each behavior.

A	B	C	D
Leadership Interactions	How often does your team leader do this?	How well does your team leader do this?	How often is your team leader's interaction appropriate to your work-related needs?*
	Rarely 1 2 3 4 5 Often	Needs Improvement 1 2 3 4 5 Well	Rarely 1 2 3 4 5 Often
STYLE IV			
a) Delegates tasks and allows you to work and make decisions on your own.	1 2 3 4 5	1 2 3 4 5	1 2 3 4 5
b) Allows you to set your own pace and to determine ways to accomplish your tasks.	1 2 3 4 5	1 2 3 4 5	1 2 3 4 5
c) There is little or no day-to-day interaction about your task.	1 2 3 4 5	1 2 3 4 5	1 2 3 4 5
d) Interaction on your task is mainly factual.	1 2 3 4 5	1 2 3 4 5	1 2 3 4 5
e) Allows you to exercise your talents and attain your own standards of performance.	1 2 3 4 5	1 2 3 4 5	1 2 3 4 5
TOTAL (Add the numbers that you circled in each column)			

*Your work-related needs might include training, role modeling, coaching, encouragement, feedback on performance, delegation, negotiation, collaboration, teamwork, and listening. You may want to specify which ones you are referring to by circling them here. Add others if appropriate.

Feedback to Your Team Leader About Your Creativity at Work

Your Team Leader's Name and Job Title:_____

a) Please list what you like about your team leader's interactions with you:

b) Please list things your team leader does that help you to increase your creativity at work:

c) Please list things that would help you increase your creativity at work if your team leader were to do them more frequently or more skillfully (please specify which):

d) Please list things that would help you increase your creativity at work if your team leader were to do them less frequently or to stop doing them (please specify which):

e) Please list what you want improved in your team leader's interactions with you:

Scoring

Add up the numbers circled in columns B, C, and D separately for each style and record the totals in the indicated spaces.

Interpretation for Team Leader

1. COLUMN B: A score of 20 or above in this column indicates you use this style a great deal. A score of 12 or less indicates you may want to consider using this style more often. Remember, most people have one strong style with a secondary backup style.

2. COLUMN C: A score of 20 or above in this column indicates you probably are very skillful in this style. Scores of 12 or below indicate you may want to consider developing your skills in this style. Behaviors marked 1 or 2 in column C indicate a need for change or more training, but only you can decide if this is true.

3. COLUMN D: A score of 20 or above in this column indicates you use this style appropriately to meet the work-related needs of the people in your work group with respect to their willingness (motivation), ability, confidence, and performance level. A score of 12 or less indicates you may want to consider developing greater awareness and sensitivity to your team's needs. Interactions marked 1 or 2 in column D are red flags that can lead to team member resentment and lower creativity and productivity.

Responding to the Team

Respond to the feedback from your work group in a way that (a) increases trust in you, (b) improves the overall creativity of your team for excellence and renewal, (c) raises its motivation to be more creative, and (d) will improve your leadership flexibility and effectiveness. For example, you might call a meeting of your work group, thank the members for their cooperation, reveal what you learned, then plan ways with them to improve the quality of the creative climate, to raise the creativity of the work group for excellence and renewal, and to improve the quality of the interactions among you.

Action Steps for the Team Leader

In addition to the suggestions in the interpretation section, Tables A-1 and A-2 offer help in developing various leadership styles.

Table A-1. Cycle Your Leadership Interactions to Help Self-Direction

By matching your leadership behaviors to the level of self-direction for each specific task, you can help people in your work group become more self-directed and more self-motivated to be creative for excellence and renewal.

	NEW PERSON NEW TASK				SELF-DIRECTED TEAM OR PERSON		
Leadership Style	Directive Style	→	Participative Style	→	Catalytic Style	→	Non-Directive Style
Predominant Behaviors	Telling Asserting Modeling	→	Coaching Negotiating Collaborating	→	Encouraging Facilitating Listening	→	Delegating

From: Glassman, E. (1986). Managing for creativity: Back to basics in R&D. *R&D Management, 16*: 176-183.

Table A-2. When to Use Each Leadership Style

When the person's ability to do the task is:	Low ↓	Moderate ↓	High ↓	High ↓
And when the person's willingness to do the task is:	Low ↓	Moderate ↓	High ↓	High ↓
And when the person's performance level on the task is:	Low ↓	Moderate ↓	High ↓	High ↓
And when the person's confidence to do the task unsupervised is:	Low ↓	Low ↓	Moderate ↓	High ↓
Then use the:	Directive Style	Participative Style	Catalytic Style	Non-Directive Style
With its predominant behaviors	Telling Asserting Modeling Structuring	Coaching Negotiating Collaborating	Encouraging Facilitating Listening	Delegating

From: Glassman, E. (1986). Managing for creativity: Back to basics in R&D. *R&D Management, 16*: 176-183.

Appendix C

Spoilers of On-the-Job Creativity in Your Work Group

Please check those creativity spoilers that exist in your team:

_____Negative reactions: Negative people are likely to be very creative and imaginative in poking holes in other people's new ideas. Often this type of destructive imagination is amazingly adept at generating objection after objection right out of the blue. Creative low-conformers can do this wonderfully.

_____Conformity (fitting in): Well-developed habits; well-developed technology; well-developed thoughts; a preoccupation with tradition.

_____Self-discouragement: Doubts that one is creative; fear of failure (produce or perish); fear of looking foolish; fear of not fitting in; modesty and self-effacement; fear of seeming to be different; timidity; shyness; pride.

_____Secrecy: New facts stimulate creative thought.

_____Quick creativity spoilers: "Why something new now?" "If it ain't broke, don't fix it." "We don't need new ideas around here." "We considered that idea five years ago." "They (we) already tried that." "If it were any good, someone else (our competitors) would have thought of it."

_____Reward system generates pressure for immediate results.

_____Not using the creative potential in people because it is not in their job description.

_____Certainty, dogmatism, and negativity from experts not trained to help creativity. Reluctance to be spontaneous and play "what if" or "let's pretend."

_____The Myth of the Creativity Mountain Top:

- Creativity is a mysterious ability of a few gifted people.
- Creativity is a mystical act.
- Creativity is generating new ideas out of nothing.
- Creativity always happens with a big bang.

_____An inability to change mind funnels.

List other creativity spoilers in your work group here:

Action Steps

Using the Creativity Procedures you have learned in this book, find ways to reduce the creativity spoilers you checked in the above list.

Appendix D

Help Creativity in Your Work Group

Please check those that would be helpful to you and your work group.

_____Defer judgement and postpone evaluation. Avoid quick negative criticism.

_____Help each new idea with I.P.N.C.,"Yes, if...," and I.I.A. prior to exercising critical judgement.

_____Avoid early commitment to an idea. Don't settle for mundane solutions. Purge immediate solutions and avoid the quick fix to solve a problem. Use forced relationships to generate novel ideas.

_____Use metaphors and analogies involving animals, plants, Martians, Jovians, Venusians, history, primitive tribes, etc., to stimulate creativity.

_____Use advanced idea-generating procedures, like brainstorming, brainwriting, non-evaluative listing, free word association imagery, future fantasy.

_____Structure the problem-solving process so that it emphasizes the three key creative steps: Defining problems; generating ideas; selecting and combining creative ideas into creative trigger-proposals, workable solutions, and practical action plans.

_____Tell people in your work group that you want them to be creative and solve problems in new ways.

_____Help new ideas; listen non-evaluatively. Use the art of positive noncommittal, such as: "Interesting. Let's hear more."

_____Accommodate to the low conforming creative person in your work group.

_____Help absorb the risks creative people in your work group take.

_____Give everyone in the work group time so the incubation phase of the creative process will give rise to the illumination phase. Allow people to stay away from the office. Remove the stigma associated with thinking time. Provide sabbaticals and mini-vacations for people.

_____Introduce training programs on advanced Creativity Procedures, creative problem solving and team effectiveness.

_____Trust intuition. Give half-developed ideas a chance; take intuitive leaps and make gut decisions, use prods to the imagination; take action quickly on new ideas rather than delay; try out half-baked ideas.

_____Recruit and hire creative people for your work group, people who are intrinsically motivated to solve problems because of the challenge; people who are low-conforming and not inhibited by ordinary constraints; people who are not afraid to risk.

_____Move your leadership style toward flexibility and accommodation.

_____Ask for volunteers rather than assigning people in your work group new tasks.

_____Reduce internal blocks in yourself. Reduce your critical thinking about your own ideas. Choose the best environment to foster creativity for yourself. Use structured, focused techniques. Use analogies and metaphors. Play, have fun. Enjoy work. You deserve it.

_____Encourage creative expression; postpone critical expression.

_____Get rid of your creativity-spoiling habits: self-criticism; anxiety; your need for approval; premature evaluation; avoiding the unknown; listening to evaluate; following tradition; avoiding risks; making unwarranted assumptions; your need for predictability; your need to be right all the time, rather than helpful; your need to appear responsible and dependable all the time.

_____Engage in the deliberate, relentless generation of alternative ways of looking at things (establish a daily quota for new ideas).

_____Challenge assumed boundaries and unwarranted assumptions with "Why?" questions.

_____Risk being wrong by deferring judgment. Give up the need to be right all the time; be helpful rather than right when needed.

_____Foster and encourage intrinsic motivation in yourself and in others. Focus on the daily enjoyment of work, rather than on long-term rewards.

_____When nothing else works, try something counterintuitive or bizarre.

_____Use an Idea Gallery outside your office door to gather additional ideas on ways to increase creativity.

_____Help the low-conforming person who is uninhibited by ordinary constraints.

_____When faced with the obvious, look elsewhere (Charlie Chan).

Action Step

When all members of your team have checked this list, make a list of those items most frequently checked and post it in your meeting room. Refer to it when you need help in being creative.

Appendix E

How Well Do You Help
On-the-Job Creativity?

Please circle the number that indicates how much you support and encourage the creative efforts of people in your work group.

	Low				High
1. Your focus on their self-motivation and responsible self-direction.	1	2	3	4	5
2. Your interest in their ideas (I.P.N.C.)	1	2	3	4	5
3. A fair hearing for their ideas or suggestions (I.I.A.).	1	2	3	4	5
4. Your encouragement for them to innovate on the job.	1	2	3	4	5
5. Intrinsic rewards for creativity or innovating on the job.	1	2	3	4	5
6. Encouragement of diverse opinions among the members of your work group.	1	2	3	4	5
7. Confidence to tell you about the mistakes they make.	1	2	3	4	5
8. Responsibility given to do the job right.	1	2	3	4	5
9. Your avoidance of the quick fix during discussions.	1	2	3	4	5
10. Trusting them to do the job without always checking on them.	1	2	3	4	5
11. Opportunity for them to volunteer for other jobs.	1	2	3	4	5
12. Your dealing easily with confusion, disorder, and chaos.	1	2	3	4	5

13. Your adjustment of your leadership style to the situation.　　1　2　3　4　5

14. Your openness to receive their opinion of how you might improve your own performance on the job.　　1　2　3　4　5

15. Your standard for judging your own performance.　　1　2　3　4　5

16. Your encouragement of idea submissions during meetings.　　1　2　3　4　5

17. Your enthusiasm for the work you all are engaged in.　　1　2　3　4　5

18. Their freedom to learn from their own mistakes.　　1　2　3　4　5

19. Their enthusiasm for the work they are engaged in.　　1　2　3　4　5

20. The extent to which you allow members of your work group to set their own goals for their job.　　1　2　3　4　5

21. The number of rules and regulations you have.　　1　2　3　4　5

22. Your avoidance of quick negative criticism.　　1　2　3　4　5

On a separate page, write ideas on how to improve on-the-job creativity in your work group.

Scoring

Total the scores that you circled. Your lowest possible total is 22; the highest possible, 110.

Action Steps

If your score is 88 or higher, you perceive yourself as very supportive of creative efforts. The next step would be to ask the other members of your team for their perceptions. If your self-score is below 88, look at the items that you marked with a score of less than 4 and work on ways to overcome these tendencies.

Appendix F

A Questionnaire to Assess Your Team's Creativity Potential

A number of factors have been shown to affect creativity. In order to assess these factors, please evaluate your work group with respect to each of the statements on the following pages using the five-point scale below. Going through this activity should give you insights into changes you should implement.

DIRECTIONS: Circle the number that you think applies to your team.

0. We never do this.

1. We rarely do this.

2. We sometimes do this.

3. We frequently do this.

5. We always do this.

(Please note there is no rating of 4.)

A. CLIMATE AND HABITS

		Never	Sometimes		Always
1.	We buffer people from interruptions, ceremonial functions, and unnecessary meetings.	0	1	2	3	5
2.	We encourage the exchange of ideas.	0	1	2	3	5
3.	We are told explicitly when creativity is wanted.	0	1	2	3	5
√ 4.	We help new ideas flourish rather than play devil's advocate. We avoid quick negative criticism and an automatic "No" when we hear new ideas and proposals.	0	1	2	3	5
5.	We deliberately avoid assuming boundaries and making unwarranted assumptions that box us in during creativity sessions.	0	1	2	3	5
√ 6.	We allocate enough time to creative thinking, to incubation time, and to using Creativity Procedures.	0	1	2	3	5
7.	We state positive things about a new idea or proposal before we state the difficulties that have to be overcome.	0	1	2	3	5
8. √	Creativity is an ongoing, on-the-job activity that everyone is encouraged to do for excellence and renewal.	0	1	2	3	5
9.	Individuals are encouraged to exhibit spontaneity and humor.	0	1	2	3	5
√10.	We discuss how the climate and habits in the team affect our creativity.	0	1	2	3	5
√11.	We encourage people to take risks and do not punish them for expected failure. We learn from failure.	0	1	2	3	5
12.	We value "thinking time" as well as "doing things."	0	1	2	3	5

Total for Part A
(Add the numbers inside the circles.)

B. CREATIVITY PROCEDURES

	Never	Sometimes			Always

1. We use analogies, metaphors, and forced combinations to help generate novel ideas.   0   1   2   3   5

2. We use a variety of procedures in addition to brainstorming to enhance idea generation.   0   1   2   3   5

3. We generate criteria to select ideas after idea generation, not before.   0   1   2   3   5

4. We discuss how Creativity Procedures help or spoil our creativity.   0   1   2   3   5

5. We encourage the generation of bizarre ideas and use them to trigger better ideas.   0   1   2   3   5

6. We select and combine ideas creatively before we generate sensible, workable solutions.   0   1   2   3   5

7. We use a variety of procedures to define problems before we generate ideas for solutions.   0   1   2   3   5

8. We set quotas for new ideas before we generate and select them.   0   1   2   3   5

9. We postpone evaluation and defer judgement when we are generating ideas to solve a problem.   0   1   2   3   5

10. We use idea-generating procedures, such as brainstorming, brainwriting, forced combinations, and future fantasy.   0   1   2   3   5

11. We separate defining problems, generating ideas, and combining ideas into three separate steps during problem solving.   0   1   2   3   5

12. Everyone obtains ongoing training in Creativity Procedures and in helping the creative climate.   0   1   2   3   5

Total for Part B
(Add the numbers inside the circles)

C. WORK GROUP

		Never	Sometimes		Always
1.	Deadlines are set to allow plenty of time for creative thinking.	0	1	2 3	5
2.	We have a creativity room with materials for tinkering, thinking, and planning creatively.	0	1	2 3	5
√3.	We obtain outside stimulation by scheduling seminars by experts in areas other than our own.	0	1	2 3	5
4.	People are encouraged to seek resource help elsewhere if they cannot find resources to help new ideas or proposals within the team.	0	1	2 3	5
5.	Help is provided to develop ideas and proposals for review by others.	0	1	2 3	5
6.	We look carefully at creative job applicants even if their applications are written in pencil and only half-filled out.	0	1	2 3	5
√7.	We discuss how our structures help or spoil creativity for excellence and renewal.	0	1	2 3	5
8.	Our performance reviews encourage risky creative efforts, ideas, and actions.	0	1	2 3	5
√9.	We have separate incentive systems for low- and high-conforming creative people.	0	1	2 3	5
△10.	We attend training programs on Creativity Procedures, creative problem solving and team effectiveness.	0	1	2 3	5
√11.	We have a system to give quick approval to new ideas and the resources to test or implement them.	0	1	2 3	5
√12.	We fill and renew our minds with new information for creativity by attending professional meetings, trade fairs, visiting customers, etc.	0	1	2 3	5

don't say no

Total for Part C
(Add the numbers inside the circles.)

D. LEADER'S HELP

		Never	*Sometimes*		*Always*

1. Leaders use participative performance appraisals based on mutually set goals and objectives.   0 1 2 3 5

✓ 2. Disagreements and disputes are resolved by consensus negotiation rather than by edict.   0 1 2 3 5

3. We discuss how our leader helps or spoils our creativity.   0 1 2 3 5

✓ 4. Leaders help people move toward independence and responsible self-direction.   0 1 2 3 5

5. Supervision is not too tight or too loose.   0 1 2 3 5

6. Leaders encourage people to exercise their talents and attain their own standards of performance.   0 1 2 3 5

7. Leaders allow people to determine how to accomplish objectives.   0 1 2 3 5

✓ 8. People are encouraged to make decisions and solve problems on their own.   0 1 2 3 5

9. Leaders solicit and help new ideas.   0 1 2 3 5

✓ 10. Leaders are flexible and accommodating to individual work-related needs.   0 1 2 3 5

✓ 11. Leaders match style to the needs of the situation.   0 1 2 3 5

12. Leaders encourage and require on-the-job creativity for excellence and renewal.   0 1 2 3 5

_____

Total for Part D
(Add the numbers inside the circles)

E. MEETINGS

		Never	Sometimes		Always

1. During meetings we defer judgment on new ideas and avoid early commitment to an idea until we have lots of ideas to choose from.   0 1 2 3 5

2. Our meetings are designed to allow people to freewheel, brainstorm, and generate bizarre trigger ideas.   0 1 2 3 5

3. All members contribute ideas during meetings.   0 1 2 3 5

4. During meetings, our energy level is high.   0 1 2 3 5

5. In meetings, people talk about the positive aspects of an idea before the negatives. We help a new idea flourish before it is subjected to critical thinking.   0 1 2 3 5

6. During meetings, there is much spontaneity and humor.   0 1 2 3 5

7. We discuss how we help or spoil creativity during meetings of the team.   0 1 2 3 5

8. We make decisions by consensus.   0 1 2 3 5

9. Ideas are shared openly and freely during meetings.   0 1 2 3 5

10. During meetings, the position of chair is rotated among members.   0 1 2 3 5

11. We solve problems using Creativity Procedures during meetings.   0 1 2 3 5

12. During meetings, we form small groups to quickly generate problem statements and ideas to solve problems.   0 1 2 3 5

_____

Total for Part E
(Add the numbers inside the circles.)

F. MOTIVATION FOR CREATIVITY AND RISK

		Never	*Sometimes*		*Always*

1. The incentives and rewards for creativity are designed to enhance the motivation to be creative again. 0 1 2 3 5

2. People are encouraged to intrinsically motivate themselves to be creative. 0 1 2 3 5

3. Emphasis is on the daily enjoyment and challenge of the work rather than on long-term rewards. 0 1 2 3 5

4. We encourage people to intrinsically motivate themselves to solve problems because of the challenge and daily enjoyment. 0 1 2 3 5

5. Rewards in the team are fair. 0 1 2 3 5

6. People are allowed to volunteer for assignments. 0 1 2 3 5

7. People are encouraged to become involved in the challenge of the work, the enjoyment and pleasure in the process, the total immersion in the activity, and the joy of solution. 0 1 2 3 5

8. There is a high stability of employment. 0 1 2 3 5

9. People work for self-satisfaction. 0 1 2 3 5

10. There is a wide choice of rewards for a successful creative effort. 0 1 2 3 5

11. People are encouraged to learn from failure, not punished for it. 0 1 2 3 5

12. We discuss how effectively we motivate for creativity and risk in our team. 0 1 2 3 5

Total for Part F
(Add the numbers inside the circles.)

G. TOLERANCE FOR LOW CONFORMITY

		Never	*Sometimes*	*Always*
1.	There is a high level of tolerance for borderline behavior.	0 1	2 3	5
2.	People are encouraged to respect different life styles.	0 1	2 3	5
3.	People are encouraged to express ideas outside the mainstream thinking of the team.	0 1	2 3	5
4.	There is a high level of tolerance for humor.	0 1	2 3	5
5.	The social graces of loners, extroverts, introverts, and innovators are accommodated in the team.	0 1	2 3	5
6.	Individuals are encouraged to decorate and individualize their offices as much as possible.	0 1	2 3	5
7.	Individuals are encouraged to dress as they wish.	0 1	2 3	5
8.	Team members are encouraged to utilize the unique strengths of other people and to ignore differences that do not relate to work effectiveness.	0 1	2 3	5
9.	We discuss how our tolerance for deviancy helps or spoils creativity.	0 1	2 3	5
10.	We encourage low-conforming behavior, ideas, and proposals.	0 1	2 3	5
11.	Beards, moustaches, and hair styles are not an issue in the team.	0 1	2 3	5
12.	We value the creative low-conforming person and the creative high-conforming person, and we accommodate to both types.	0 1	2 3	5

Total for Part G
(Add the numbers inside the circles.)

Messages to Your Team
About Your Creativity at Work:

1. Please list what you like about your team's interactions with you:

2. Please list things your team does that help to increase your creativity at work:

3. Please list things that would help you increase your creativity at work if your team were to do them more frequently or more skillfully (please specify which):

4. Please list things that would help you increase your creativity at work if your team were to do them less frequently or stop doing them (please specify which):

5. Please list what you want improved in your team's interactions with you:

Creativity-Potential Profile

In each part of the preceding instrument, add the numbers that you circled and write the total in the space provided at the bottom of each part. Then transfer these totals to the appropriate spaces in the following matrix. Then write in the grand total for all the parts.

Part	Total
A. Climate and Habits	
B. Creativity Procedures	
C. Work Group	
D. Leader's Help	
E. Meetings	
F. Motivation	
G. Tolerance	
Total of all Parts	

relax

If the grand total is over 400, either congratulate yourself and keep up the good work or go back and make sure you answered the questions honestly. Now look at the score for each part and notice which ones are lowest. Review the questions for those sections and make an action plan to increase the scores.

Appendix G

More Creativity Spoilers

Here is a list of the creativity-spoiling habits. CHECK THOSE YOU WOULD LIKE TO STOP DOING:

_____Not enough time is allotted to the incubation phase of the creative process.

_____People are not deliberately encouraged to increase the number of diverse elements in their mind.

_____We do not deliberately misperceive the world to obtain a creative viewpoint.

_____We think we are not creative.

_____We do not let ourselves act spontaneously even for a minute.

_____We do not deliberately search out alternative mind funnels.

_____Early ideas for solving a problem have to be fair.

_____We make unwarranted assumptions about problems too easily and do not check them out, even if we are aware we are doing this.

_____The quick fix is accepting the first adequate solution to a problem, thereby denying our creative ability to find a better solution.

_____We rush to generate solutions before defining problems or do not examine alternative mind funnels to make sure we are working on the right problem.

_____We do not search enough within a single mind funnel for the entire range of possible new ideas and solutions within it.

_____We do not explore new ideas for additional new mind funnels that could lead to more ideas.

_____We do not allot enough time to explore different mind funnels.

_____We often assume boundaries that do not exist. We stay within the lines. We think within the rules. We do *not* check them out with others.

_____We respond to new ideas with quick negative criticism and a habitual automatic "No" that usually kills new ideas and spoils creativity.

_____We discourage and squelch new ideas, especially bizarre ideas and impossible intermediates.

_____We expect sellers of ideas to present their ideas in perfect form. No half-developed ideas for us. Every "i" dotted, every "t" crossed, every concept clear, every label and term used correctly, and no errors in spelling or grammar.

_____We accept the idea stifler and allow others to shoot down ideas and spoil creativity. We do the same to our own ideas.

_____We rush to generate solutions before we adequately examine and define the problem.

_____We box in our creativity by determining criteria before we generate problem statements or ideas.

_____We do not use appropriate structured procedures to define problems creatively.

_____We turn the problem pyramid upside down and rush to generate solutions before properly defining the problem and establishing a good base on which to generate ideas.

_____We often use low-conformers when high-conformers would be more appropriate, and vice versa.

_____We evaluate ideas prematurely during meetings and do not practice non-evaluative listening.

_____We continue to carry out creativity-spoiling habits even after we know how counterproductive they are.

_____We focus on external rewards to motivate at work and devalue the intrinsic reasons to do something.

_____We allow long-range rewards to distract us from the immediate enjoyment of being creative. We allow external motivators to overpower intrinsic motivation. We distract others as well.

_____Leaders do not adjust their style to meet the work-related needs of their team for on-the-job creativity.

Action Steps

List on newsprint and post at next team meeting the items that your team members most frequently checked. Use the list to remind you to stop spoiling your creativity. Also convert the negative statements on your list into positive statements and post that version at some of your meetings.

Appendix H

Work With Your Team

Work with your team in groups of five or six. Design a team whose goal is to *spoil* creativity, listing various means you could employ:

When you have shared these, and vowed not to be like that, get together in the same groups and design a team whose goal is to *spoil* the creativity of other people in the organization, listing again the various strategies:

Discuss all these and vow not to be like that either.

Now fill out and discuss the following pages with your work group. Please be sure that when you all finish, everyone has two action plans, one for themselves and one for the team.

Define the Problems in Your Work Group

Stimulate Creativity in Your Team for Excellence and Renewal

What I Like	What I Want Improved (Make These How-To Statements)
	How to...
	How to...
	How to...
	How to...
	How to...
	How to...
	How to...
	How to...
	How to...
	How to...
	How to...
	How to...

Develop a Quick Response with Resources to Test New Ideas

1. Ways your work group provides quick resources to test or implement new ideas that you would like to improve are...

2. Suggestions for which you would be prepared to be involved are...

3. Suggestions worth considering by others are...

Stimulate Endeavor for Excellence and Renewal

4. Three ways you would evaluate improvements in innovative output are...

5. Aspects of the work climate that influence the innovativeness of your work group are...

6. Things you do that spoil creative ideas or innovation in the work group are...

7. Things people outside your work group do that spoil creative ideas or innovation of your team are...

8. Things members of your work group do that spoil creative ideas or innovation of others are...

9. Things you need to improve about yourself to be a person that helps creative ideas or innovation in your work group are...

10. Things you would change to help creative ideas in your work group are...

11. Ways creative ideas of your work group could be rewarded are...

12. Ways new ideas of your work group could be helped with resources for quick testing are...

13. Ways people in your company could actively help the creative ideas of your work group are...

Appendix I

Ready, Set, Action Plans

As all of us know, very little is carried out unless you write a specific action plan with detailed action steps containing what is to be done: who does it, when, where, and why.

This step is crucial to help on-the-job creativity for excellence and renewal. Consequently, make out an action plan using the form here. Fill it out alone or with members of your team. The sooner the better, before you forget this entirely—as you know you will if you don't write the action plan NOW. If you made action plans for each appendix, summarize them here.

Don't forget that on-the-job creativity is a probabilities game. Increase the probabilities that your work group will generate useful ideas by changing the climate and your habits, by using Creativity Procedures, by individualizing the work environment with motivating catalysts, by being flexible and using the right leadership style, by allowing intrinsic motivation to operate, etc. The payoff in excellence and renewal for your work group will make all this effort worthwhile.

Date:_____

Action Plans

Action Plan Regarding:_____

	ACTION Step 1.	*ACTION* Step 2.	*ACTION* Step 3.	*ACTION* Step 4.
What is to be done?				
Who does it?				
When?				
Where?				
Why?				
What else?				

References
and Further Readings

Adams, J. L. (1979). *Conceptual blockbusting: A guide to better ideas.* New York: W. W. Norton and Co.

Amabile, T. M. (1983). *The social psychology of creativity.* New York: Springer-Verlag.

de Bono, E. (1970). *Lateral thinking: Creativity step-by-step.* New York: Harper & Row.

Campbell, D. (1977). *Take the road to creativity and get off your dead end.* Allen, Texas: Argus Communications.

Delbecq, A. L., Van de Ven, A. H., & Gustafson, D. H. (1975). *Group techniques for program planning: A guide to nominal group and delphi processes.* Glenview, IL: Scott, Foresman.

Glassman, E. (1990). *For presidents only: Unlocking the creative potential of your management team.* New York: American Management Association. (*The Creativity Factor: Unlocking the potential of your team* is a revised edition of this book.)

Osborn, A. F. (1963). *Applied imagination* (3rd ed.). New York: Charles Scribner's.

Peters, T. & Austin, N. (1985). *A passion for excellence: The leadership difference.* New York: Random House.

Pinchot, G. (1985). *Intrapreneuring: Why you don't have to leave the corporation to become an entrepreneur.* New York: Harper & Row.

Prince, G. M. (1970). *The practice of creativity.* New York: Harper & Row.

Stein, M. I. (1975). *Stimulating creativity* (Vol. 2: *Group procedures*). New York: Academic Press.

Van Grundy, A. B. (1981). *Techniques of structured problem solving.* New York: Van Nostrand Reinhold.

Waterman, R. H. (1987). *The renewal factor.* New York: Bantam.